The
CLASSIC
SLOW
COOKER

The CLASSIC SLOW COOKER

BEST-LOVED FAMILY RECIPES to Make FAST and COOK SLOW

JUDY HANNEMANN

THE COUNTRYMAN PRESS · WOODSTOCK, VT.

Photo Credits:

All photography courtesy of the author unless otherwise noted.

The Countryman Press
www.countrymanpress.com

A division of W. W. Norton & Company, Inc.
500 Fifth Avenue, New York, NY 10110
www.wwnorton.com

978-1-58157-372-5

10 9 8 7 6 5 4 3 2 1

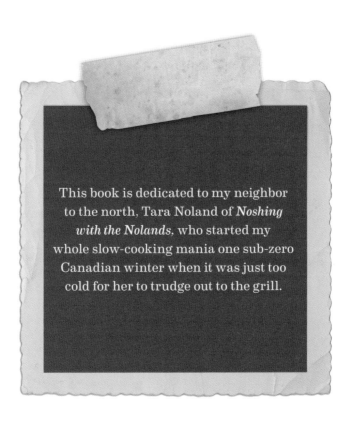

This book is dedicated to my neighbor to the north, Tara Noland of *Noshing with the Nolands,* who started my whole slow-cooking mania one sub-zero Canadian winter when it was just too cold for her to trudge out to the grill.

Contents

INTRODUCTION 10

CHOOSING A SLOW COOKER 12

1. APPETIZERS
Asian Orange Chicken Wings 18
Aloha Pineapple Sauce 19
Smoky Pimento Cheese Queso Dip with
    Country White Croutons 20
Chex Snack Mix 23
Hot Jalapeño & Chile Popper Dip 24

2. SOUPS
Beef Barley Soup 28
Hearty Northeast Bean Soup 31
Cheeseburger Soup 33
Smoked Sausage & Lentil Soup 35
Steak & Ale Cheese Soup 36
Split Pea Soup with Ham 38

3. CHICKEN
Maple-Kissed Roasted Chicken 42
Roasted Drumsticks...................... 44
Creole Seasoning Blend 45
Cheesy Bacon Chicken & Taters 47
Chicken Stroganoff...................... 48
Chicken & Noodles....................... 49
Chicken with Creamy Mushroom Rice 50
Chicken with Vegetables 52
Ranch Seasoning Mix 53
Fruity BBQ Chicken 54
Teriyaki Chicken 56

4. PORK
Juicy Maple Pork with Sweet Potatoes 60
Maple & Sage Seasoning Rub.............. 61
Apple Butter BBQ Ribs 62
Brown Sugar Country-Style Pork Ribs 64
Mississippi Ribs........................67
Cheese and Potato Stuffed Pork Chops 68
Calypso Pork Chops 71
Pork Chop Stroganoff....................72
Pork Chops with Golden Ranch Gravy 74
Cheesy Sausage & Taters 75

5. BEEF

Classic Pot Roast 79
Classic Pot Roast with Veggies 80
Roasted Beef 83
Asian BBQ Beef Strips 85
Braised Short Ribs 87
Maple-Glazed Short Ribs 89
Cream & Ale Short Ribs 91
Fruited Short Ribs 92
Beef Stroganoff 94
Braised Steak 97
Ginger Beef with Mandarin Oranges 99
Chopped Steak with Onion Mushroom Gravy 101
Swiss Steak 102
Mississippi Swiss Steak 105
Orange Beef with Fire Peppers 106
Sichuan Beef with Carrots 109
Stuffed Beef Rolls 110
Maple Meatloaf 113
Chili Hater's Chili 114

6. PASTA

Baked Ziti 119
Five-Cheese Lasagna 121
Spaghetti & Meat Sauce 123
Creamy Penne 124

7. SIDES

Candied Acorn Squash 128
Candied Baby Carrots 129
Citrus Greek Potatoes 131
Hot German Potato Salad 133
Cheesy Hashbrown Casserole 134
Spicy Roasted Chili Cheese Fries 136
Roasted Chile Sauce 138
Cheesy Ranch Potatoes 139
Slow Cooker Baked Potatoes 141

8. SWEET TREATS

Apple Pie Cake 145
Apple Dapple Pudding 146
Banana Bread 148
Cherry Cobbler 151
Tropical Ambrosia Dump Cake 152
Chocolate Cherry Cobbler 154
Blueberry Cobbler 157
Donut Bread Pudding 159
Lemon Bars 160
Dulce de Leche 163
Mom's Rice Pudding 164
Slow Cooker Brownies 165
Peanut Butter Cup Trifle 166
Peanut Butter Caramel Sauce 167

INDEX 168

Acknowledgments

I would like to thank the following folks,
without whose help this work would never have been possible:

LISA SUMMERS
Creole Contessa

KATERINA DELIDIMOU
Culinary Flavors

CLAUDIA LAMASCOLO
What's Cookin' Italian Style

GINNY McMEANS
Vegan in the Freezer

MELISSA SPERKA
Melissa's Southern Style Kitchen

MELISSA HAYDON
Served Up with Love

KRISTA MARSHALL
Everyday Mom's Meals

SARAH OLSON
The Magical Slow Cooker

LAUREEN KING
Art and the Kitchen

RONDA EAGLE
Kitchen Dreaming

VERONICA GANTLEY
My Catholic Kitchen

RAYFORD & LAURA TAYLOR
my favorite business advisors

STAN & LINDA LEMONS
my fearless taste testers

Introduction

I wasn't always a fan of slow cookers, or of anything slow-cooked. First of all, my mother never owned a slow cooker, and my family, with the exception of my father, didn't really care for dishes that were stewy or "cooked all day." My mom was more or less a baking and grilling type of cook.

The first slow cooker I owned was one of those 3-quart round affairs with an irremovable crock. I was married by that time and my new husband, unlike me and my family, was a fan of stews and dishes that cooked all day.

Fast-forwarding a bit here, the saga of my first foray into slow cooking was not a success. Everything was an even-brown color that fell apart and didn't taste so good. Even my husband, the stew fan, said that the food had a weird taste—especially the onions. So I ended up giving the appliance to a neighbor.

A few years later I bought a larger model with a removable crock for easy cleaning. Don't ask me why I bought this. The only explanation I can give is that I'm an incurable kitchen-appliance junkie. However, this time I had some success, in that there was a recipe in the little booklet that came with the cooker for a smoked brisket that my husband loved and I didn't mind either. But that's all we used it for, except for the occasional split pea soup.

It wasn't until many years later that I discovered the versatility of the slow cooker. My sister absolutely loved hers and would cook most meals in it. She'd bake with hers as well, and that got me to wondering whether I'd missed out on some secret for using the appliance.

But what really lit my slow cooker fire was a recipe post from a wonderful Canadian food blogger I am friendly with, Tara Noland of *Noshing with the Nolands.* Tara lives in Alberta, and it gets cold up there . . . *really* cold. In one post, she shared with readers that her family had been begging for barbecued chicken; she wanted to oblige but couldn't bear trudging out to her gas grill in minus-40-degree temps. So she made barbecued chicken in her slow cooker. The end result, as pictured on her blog, looked amazingly delicious.

After I read her post and scrolled through her photographs, I really wanted to experiment with the slow-cooking process. So I turned my kitchen into a laboratory of sorts. I discovered that not all food cooked in this appliance has to be some tossed-together nondescript stew. You can produce gourmet-style food just by adding an extra step or two to the process, which is why a lot of my recipes are not of the dump-and-go variety.

And now? You couldn't part me from my slow cooker. I'm so much of a fan that I own four. Yes, *four*, in different shapes and sizes.

I hope you will love this collection of recipes as much as I do!

CHOOSING A SLOW COOKER

Slow cookers come in many shapes and sizes as well as analog and digital, so how do you know which one is right for you?

As far as brands go, there are a range of slow cookers are on the market, and all the major manufacturers offer a warranty.

If you are away all day, I'd definitely recommend a digital model that automatically switches to low after the cook time. Of course, the fancier the features, the higher the cost. There are now Wi-Fi-enabled slow cookers that allow you to remotely program the cooker via a smart phone or other device. Since I'm now retired and am generally home all day, my choice is the humble analog cookers with the dial you set manually. I also find that the less bells and whistles you have, the less that can go wrong with the machine—but that's the engineer in me.

SIZE

When it comes to size, you should take into account how the cooker will be used and how many people you will be serving. Keep in mind that cooking times given in recipes are based on a cooker that is at least half full but not more than two-thirds full. If it's less than half full, it will cook faster. Conversely, if it's more than two-thirds full, it will cook slower.

If you intend to use yours primarily for entertaining (dinner parties, buffets, etc.), then I'd say get the biggest one you can—7 quarts. There are many slow cookers designed especially for buffet use. A 7-quart cooker is an excellent choice for larger families and families with big appetites as well.

For family use, the best all-around choice would be a 6-quart model. This size would adequately serve a family of four, and you might also get another meal out of it. Smaller families might do perfectly well with a 5-quart model. It's always been the standard size, more or less, and it's also the most economical. It's my go-to size.

Singles and empty-nesters' best sizes are 3.5- to 4-quart models. If you're not big eaters, you will still have leftovers with this size. I wouldn't recommend going any smaller— there are 2-quart models available that are relatively expensive compared to the larger sizes and very limited in use.

SHAPE

My shape of choice is oval. Ovals can cook anything you want to cook, but they are perfect for roasts and many things you will want to cook in a single layer. That said, larger rectangles are great for pasta casseroles and baking, and small round crocks are perfect for smaller portions. You can also set up a few small cookers at a buffet.

Casserole crocks have an insert that is 13 x 9-inches, the standard size for a casserole baking dish. If you do a lot of casseroles, this may be the answer for you. However, be advised that its use is limited to mostly "flat" foods. You cannot cook a roast in it because the insert is too shallow. Its volume is small as well—only 3 quarts.

If you are short on storage space, a multi-cooker might be a good option. This machine functions as an oven, electric skillet, steamer, and slow cooker. It's digital, and will switch to warm after the allotted cooking time. The default cook times for the slow-cooker function are 8 hours for low and 4 hours for high. One caveat about this appliance: it generally cooks in two-thirds the time of a conventional slow cooker, which might not work for someone who spends long hours of the day away from home. Also, the insert is nonstick coated aluminum, not ceramic, as with the conventional slow cooker.

COOK TIME

All slow cookers cook differently, so times are pretty much approximate in recipes. I always advise checking a little before the minimum cooking time to test for doneness. Of my four slow cookers, three are from the same manufacturer, and they all cook differently.

APPETIZERS

ASIAN ORANGE CHICKEN WINGS

SERVES ABOUT 8

Cooking time: 3 to 4 hours on high

Wings remain one of the most popular appetizers in the United States. I remember the days when you could buy them for 10 cents per pound; too bad that's no longer the case! Since I've always been a big fan of Asian cuisine, I wondered how wings flavored like the classic Chinese American dish Orange Chicken would taste. No surprise, they're delicious. You don't need to, but marinating the wings overnight produces a superior flavor. Also, I recommend browning the wings before you put them in the slow cooker. A few minutes under the broiler is all it takes.

4 to 5 pounds chicken wings (see Note)

FOR THE MARINADE (OPTIONAL)
2 cups Aloha Pineapple Sauce (recipe follows)

FOR THE ORANGE SAUCE
1 tablespoon orange zest
4 cloves garlic, minced
½ cup dark brown sugar
½ cup frozen orange juice concentrate
¼ cup soy sauce
1½ cups water
¼ teaspoon red pepper flakes
¼ teaspoon black pepper
2 to 3 drops dark sesame oil

1 If desired, marinate wings overnight in Aloha Pineapple Sauce. Drain marinade and pat the wings dry. Place wings on broiler pan and broil for 3 to 4 minutes to brown.

2 Place wings in slow cooker. Turn to high and cook for 3 to 4 hours.

3 While wings are cooking, prepare the orange sauce. Add all sauce ingredients to a small saucepan, stir to combine, and bring to a boil over medium-high heat. Reduce heat and cook until sauce is reduced by 50 percent. Remove from heat.

4 When wings are done, drain any accumulated liquid from the crock. Pour orange sauce over the wings in the slow cooker. Turn cooker to warm setting and let wings sit for 30 minutes.

 *Note: If you are using whole fresh wings, remove the wing tips (I save them for making stock) and separate wings at joint to get 2 pieces. If using frozen chicken wing drumettes, defrost before marinating or cooking.*

ALOHA PINEAPPLE SAUCE

MAKES ABOUT 2 CUPS

This is a wonderful marinade for Asian Orange Chicken Wings (previous recipe), and it's great for steaks and grilled chicken as well. The flavor packs a punch, whether you're using it for basting or as a dipping sauce.

8 ounces pineapple juice
½ cup packed dark brown sugar
⅓ cup soy sauce
3 large garlic cloves, crushed
1 tablespoon mirin or white wine

1 Combine all ingredients in a small saucepan. Bring to boil and reduce heat to a simmer. Continue to simmer, uncovered, for about 10 to 15 minutes or until sauce is reduced by 50 percent and has a consistency like maple syrup.

2 Cool to lukewarm, then refrigerate until chilled. (If preparing recipe for a marinade, I recommend you make the sauce either very early in the day or the day before you plan to use it.)

SMOKY PIMENTO CHEESE QUESO DIP

with COUNTRY WHITE CROUTONS

SERVES ABOUT 6

Cooking time: about 2 hours on low

A favorite dip of mine from my good friend Lisa, who's also known as the Creole Contessa. I'm always telling her that she's my "dip maven," and with good reason! I'm sure you'll enjoy this cheesy and flavorful dip as much as I do.

FOR THE PIMENTO CHEESE DIP

1 jar (4 ounces) diced pimiento peppers, drained
1 jalapeño, seeded and diced
2 cups sharp Cheddar cheese, grated
1 cup smoked mozzarella, diced
1 cup jack cheese, grated
½ cup Parmesan cheese, grated
½ cup green salsa
½ cup white onion, diced
½ cup mayonnaise
½ cup sour cream
½ cup cream cheese, room temperature
2 teaspoons garlic, minced
1 teaspoon black pepper
½ teaspoon creole seasoning
½ teaspoon chili powder
Parsley to garnish

FOR THE CROUTONS

6 slices country white bread
Extra-virgin olive oil
Oregano, dried, crushed
Paprika

1. Place all the dip ingredients except parsley into slow cooker and mix well. Cook on low for about 2 hours, stirring every 20 minutes.

2. Meanwhile, make the croutons. Set the oven on broil. Cut the bread slices into quarters. Place bread pieces on baking sheet and drizzle with olive oil, then sprinkle with oregano and paprika. Broil until pieces are golden brown, then flip over and broil on other side until golden brown.

3. Assemble croutons on platter and serve with dip. Garnish with parsley.

 Recipe courtesy of www.creolecontessa.com

CHEX SNACK MIX

MAKES ABOUT 10 CUPS

Cooking time: 1 hour on low

This is the snack mix of my childhood. It dates to the late 1950s, and my memories of my mom making it for the first time are still vivid. It became my family's Saturday-night movie nibbles. Originally it was made in the oven and called for margarine, but I've updated mine to include ingredients not in the original version and of course replaced the margarine with my beloved butter.

FOR THE SNACK MIX

½ box Rice Chex (about 4 cups)
1 box Wheat Chex (about 6 cups)
3 cups any shape pretzels
½ jar (about 1 cup) lightly salted dry-roasted peanuts

FOR THE SEASONING

¼ pound (1 stick) butter, preferably unsalted, melted
1 tablespoon Worcestershire sauce
2 tablespoons soy sauce
2 teaspoons garlic powder
1 teaspoon onion powder
½ to 1 teaspoon sugar

1 Mix the cereals, pretzels, and nuts in the crock of a large (6- to 7-quart) slow cooker. (If your cooker is smaller, combine cereal mixture in a separate bowl before adding to crock.) In a small saucepan, melt the butter.

2 Stir in the Worcestershire sauce, soy sauce, garlic powder, and onion powder. Add ½ teaspoon of sugar and stir. Taste the sauce—if it is too tart, add an additional ½ teaspoon sugar (or to taste). Pour seasoning over cereal mixture and stir to coat.

3 Cover slow cooker, set to low, and heat for 1 hour, stirring every 20 minutes.

4 Spread mix on baking sheets and cool to room temperature before serving.

HOT JALAPEÑO & CHILE POPPER DIP

SERVES ABOUT 10

Cooking time: 3 hours on low

I'm crazy about hot dips—meaning they're served hot and contain hot peppers. This dip I can eat like a meal. I acquired a taste for hot dips in adulthood, since my family was not into spicy food. This one is always a hit at parties and it's usually gone within an hour!

2 packages (8 ounces each) cream cheese, cut in chunks
1 cup mayonnaise
½ cup Mexican blend shredded cheese (see Note)
½ cup grated Parmesan cheese
1 can (4 ounces) diced green chiles
1 can (4 ounces) diced jalapeños

1 Place all ingredients in a 3- or 4-quart slow cooker and mix to combine.

2 Cook on low for 3 hours, stirring every 30 minutes.

3 When dip is very warm and all cheeses melted, switch the cooker to warm setting.

4 This may be served with buttered panko bread crumbs on top—just melt 2 tablespoons of butter in a small skillet and add 1 cup of panko bread crumbs. Toss to coat and sprinkle across the top of the dip.

5 Serve with crackers or tortilla chips.

 Note: If you can't find Mexican-blend shredded cheese in your grocery store, a 1-to-1 mix of shredded sharp Cheddar and shredded Monterey Jack is a good substitute.

SOUPS

BEEF BARLEY SOUP

SERVES 2

Cooking time: 4 hours on high or 8 hours on low

This soup is a complete meal. It was my late husband's favorite, and we'd have it at least twice a month during the winter. I'd serve it with some nice crusty rolls and a green salad, depending on how hungry we were. My husband could skip the salad, but never the rolls. The soup is absolute perfection when you include them in the menu.

2 carrots, sliced
2 celery stalks, sliced
½ cup pearl barley
1 tablespoon olive oil
1 pound beef chuck roast, cut into cubes
1 teaspoon salt
½ teaspoon freshly ground black pepper
4 cups beef stock

1 Place carrots, celery, and barley in a 4- to 5-quart slow cooker.

2 In a large skillet over medium-high heat, heat the olive oil. Season the beef with salt and pepper and add to skillet, cooking 1 to 2 minutes to brown on all sides. Set skillet aside (do not wash). Transfer browned meat to the slow cooker and add 3 cups of the beef stock. Add the remaining cup of stock to the skillet and deglaze, scraping up all the browned bits into the stock. Add contents of skillet to the slow cooker and stir.

3 Cover and cook on low 8 hours, or on high 4 hours.

HEARTY NORTHEAST BEAN SOUP

2 cups dried great northern beans

3 carrots, peeled and thickly sliced

¼ cup chopped onion

1 stalk celery, sliced

½ teaspoon dried basil or about 5 large fresh basil leaves

About 3 or 4 bunches celery leaves

6 whole black peppercorns

1 cup diced kielbasa (Polish sausage or smoked sausage)

1 cup cubed smoked ham

4 cups vegetable stock

1 Cover beans with water. Soak overnight. Drain beans. Add beans to 5-quart slow cooker. Add all other ingredients to slow cooker and mix to combine.

2 Cover and cook on high for 2 hours. Reduce heat to low and cook for an addtional 10 to 12 hours or until beans are very soft and soup is thick and stew-like.

SERVES 6 TO 8

Cooking time: 2 hours on high and 10 to 12 hours on low

During a cold Northeast winter, warm and comforting soups are never far from one's thoughts. My husband and I would often call a soup such as this a meal—because it is! When I'd put this on, maybe with the leftover Easter ham bone I'd frozen, its savory scent would fill the house and all we could think about was dinnertime! This is one of those stick-to-your-ribs soups that's always a pleasure to eat.

CHEESEBURGER SOUP

SERVES 4 TO 6

Cooking time: 3 to 3½ hours on high

Who doesn't love a cheeseburger? This soup is guaranteed to please any burger lover, and it's so simple to make! It relies on some common convenience ingredients, so all you do is fill the slow cooker, set it, and forget it! This is one of the newer additions to my slow-cooking repertoire. Snuggling up on the couch with a mug of this and a good book makes for a great evening, especially when there's a chill in the air.

16 ounces (½ bag) frozen potato nuggets (like Tater Tots or Crispy Crowns)
1 pound lean ground beef
1 can (10.25 ounces) Cheddar cheese soup
1¼ cups (1 soup-can full) water
¾ cup milk
1 beef stock cube
1 tablespoon instant onion flakes, optional
2 cups Velveeta

SUGGESTED TOPPINGS
Diced bacon
Shredded Cheddar cheese
Chopped parsley

1 Place potato nuggets in the bottom of a 4- to 6-quart slow cooker.

2 Brown ground beef; drain well. Add to slow cooker.

3 Add soup, water, milk, stock cube, and onion flakes, if using. Cover and cook on high for 2 hours.

4 Add the Velveeta and cook for an additional 1 to 1½ hours on high. Stir well and serve with suggested toppings, if desired.

SMOKED SAUSAGE & LENTIL SOUP

MAKES ABOUT 10 SERVINGS

Cooking time: 5 hours on high or 8 to 10 hours on low

An old-world treat, updated. My mother-in-law used to make lentil soup all the time. It's a popular soup in her native Germany. Needless to say, it was also a favorite of my husband's. I started out making it the old-fashioned way, on the stovetop. But I soon discovered that the crock-pot method was not only easier but produced a tastier soup because of the long, slow cooking. A little bit of Germany in a bowl!

1 package (16 ounces) lentils
1 cup sliced carrots
½ cup sliced mushrooms
5 sprigs fresh thyme or ½ teaspoon dry
1 small onion, sliced
1 garlic clove, crushed
1 tub Knorr beef-concentrated stock or 2 to 3 beef stock cubes
4 whole peppercorns
1 teaspoon salt
1 pound kielbasa (or smoked sausage) sliced in ¼-inch slices
6 cups water

1 Combine all ingredients in the crock of a 5-quart (or larger) slow cooker. Cover.

2 Set to high and cook for about 5 hours (or 8 to 10 hours on low). If soup seems too thick for your taste, add a bit more water.

STEAK & ALE CHEESE SOUP

¼ cup flour
½ teaspoon salt
Pinch of black pepper
1 pound chuck or round, cut in 1-inch cubes
2 tablespoons olive oil, divided
1 small onion, sliced
½ cup sliced mushrooms
1 stalk celery, sliced
1 large garlic clove, crushed
2 large potatoes, cut in chunks
1 can (12 ounces) beer or ale
1 chicken stock cube
1 teaspoon fresh thyme, or ½ teaspoon dried
½ cup cream or evaporated milk
1½ cups shredded sharp Cheddar cheese

MAKES ABOUT 4 SERVINGS

Cooking time: 5 to 6 hours on high or 8 to 10 hours on low

This soup will remind you of eating in a small English country pub. Every time I make this, I think of the first time my mother took my sister and me to England. She was born there and wanted to show us this part of our heritage. Of course, visiting a small country pub was on the list. The pub belonged to "Aunt Sue," who was a very good friend of my eldest aunt. This was always a popular lunch at Aunt Sue's pub, which was in Aylesbury.

1 Combine flour, salt, and pepper and place in a large plastic ziplock bag. Add meat to the bag and shake until pieces are coated in flour mixture.

2 Heat 1 tablespoon of the oil in a heavy skillet over medium heat. Shake off any excess flour and place meat in hot skillet. Brown pieces on all sides, then place meat in slow cooker.

3 Return skillet to heat and add the remaining 1 tablespoon of oil. Sauté the onion, mushrooms, celery, and garlic until almost tender. Add vegetable mixture to slow cooker.

4 Add potato chunks to the slow cooker.

5 Pour beer over the beef and vegetable mixture. Add stock cube and thyme.

6 Cover and cook on high for 5 to 6 hours or low for 8 to 10 hours (I recommend cooking on high to avoid meat breaking apart).

7 Turn off cooker and add cream. Stir well. Add cheese and stir again. Replace cover and let sit for about 10 minutes. Stir again and serve.

SPLIT PEA SOUP WITH HAM

SERVES 6 TO 8

Cooking time: 6 to 8 hours on low

This soup was a tradition growing up in my home. My mom always made ham for Easter and would save the bone just for this. It was like celebrating Easter again, but this time the Easter Bunny left soup, not the usual basket of candy! Mom made this on the stovetop, but I've converted it to the slow cooker because it's the perfect method for this soup.

1 meaty ham bone or 2 cups thickly diced boneless ham

2½ cups (1 regular bag) dried split peas

1 small onion, chopped

2 carrots, sliced thickly

5 cups water (see Note)

1 bay leaf

1 teaspoon salt

5 whole peppercorns

1 sprig of fresh dill, or ⅛ teaspoon dried

1 garlic clove, crushed

1 Add all ingredients to a 5- to 6-quart slow cooker. Set on low and cook for 6 to 8 hours.

2 Serve with buttered croutons.

Note: Soup may have to be thinned with more water, depending on how your individual slow cooker cooks; 5 cups of water was about right for my cooker and produced a thick, hearty soup. If you prefer a thinner soup, use 6 cups water.

CHICKEN

MAPLE-KISSED ROASTED CHICKEN

6 large skin-on chicken thighs or 1 small whole chicken cut up

1 bag (1 pound) peeled baby carrots

Salt and pepper to taste

½ cup Maple and Sage Seasoning Rub (recipe page 61)

½ cup maple syrup

2 teaspoons Dijon mustard

SERVES 6

Cooking time: 4¼ to 6½ hours on high

Maple syrup isn't just for pancakes! I've tried it on a wide variety of foods, and in addition to being versatile, it's delicious. After using it to great effect to glaze short ribs, I decided to give it a go with chicken, and carrots seemed a natural addition—instant candied carrots! This makes for an easy and pleasing fall meal, but it's great any other time of the year as well.

1 Place chicken and baby carrots in a 4- to 6-quart slow cooker. Season with salt and pepper to taste. Sprinkle with the rub.

2 Turn slow cooker to high and cook for 4 to 6 hours. (Times vary because slow cookers do! Mine was done in $4\frac{1}{2}$ hours.)

3 Drain any liquid that accumulated in the crock.

4 In a small bowl combine maple syrup and Dijon mustard and mix well. Pour over chicken and carrots, coating evenly. Cook on high for an additional 15 to 30 minutes.

ROASTED DRUM- STICKS

SERVES 4 TO 6

Cooking time: 3 to 4 hours on high

This roasted chicken is similar to the rotisserie chicken you buy at the store, only it's cheaper and better too! I make my own spice mix for this dish, but you can use store-bought seasonings if you prefer. Even good old salt, pepper, and a dash of garlic powder would work. And you can substitute chicken thighs or breasts for the drumsticks as well. I would only caution you to monitor the pot carefully if using breasts, as they tend to dry out and become stringy with slow cooking. One other thing to note: You'll get the best results if chicken is arranged in a single layer, thus an oval slow cooker is a good idea here. You could also use 2 cookers, if you have them, to accommodate the chicken in one layer.

Note: I use my own Creole Seasoning Blend (recipe follows), but Goya's Adobo and McCormick's Rotisserie Chicken Seasoning or your favorite seasoning mix can be substituted.

3 to 4 pounds chicken drumsticks
½ cup brown sugar
1 to 2 tablespoons seasoning (see Note)

1 Spray the inside of a 5- to 7-quart slow cooker with nonstick spray. Mix together the brown sugar and seasoning blend.

2 Sprinkle seasoning over chicken pieces and rub in well. Place chicken in the bottom of the slow cooker, preferably in a single layer.

3 Cover and set to high. Cook 3 to 4 hours, or until juices run clear.

CREOLE SEASONING BLEND

MAKES ABOUT 3/4 CUP

This is the spice blend I use for Roasted Drumsticks. It has many other uses as well; I often include it in rib rubs, and it's a terrific addition to chicken salad!

2 tablespoons onion powder
2 tablespoons garlic powder
2 tablespoons oregano
2 tablespoons basil
1½ tablespoons thyme
1 tablespoon black pepper
1 tablespoon white pepper
2½ teaspoons cayenne pepper
3 tablespoons regular paprika
2 tablespoons smoky paprika
3 tablespoons kosher salt

Mix all ingredients together and store in an air-tight container.

CHEESY BACON CHICKEN & TATERS

SERVES 4 TO 6

Cooking time: 6 hours on low

This is a good and filling family meal. Easy too, just set it and forget it. The only work is in cutting up the chicken and dicing the bacon. It's also a good meal for what I call "planned overs" (make aheads), because it reheats well and the flavor improves the second time around.

1 package (32 ounces) frozen potato nuggets (like Tater Tots or Crispy Crowns) or shredded hash browns

2 boneless, skinless chicken breasts, cut in bite-sized pieces

½ cup cooked, chopped bacon, divided

2 cups shredded Cheddar cheese, divided

2 teaspoons salt

½ teaspoon pepper

¾ cup milk or cream

1 Grease well or spray the crock of a 6- to 7-quart slow cooker.

2 Place ½ of the potatoes in the bottom of the crock. Place ½ of the chicken pieces on top of the potatoes. Sprinkle ½ the bacon over the chicken. Distribute 1 cup of cheese over the top. Repeat layers once more.

3 Stir salt and pepper into milk or cream, and then pour over mixture.

4 Cover and cook for 6 hours on low.

CHICKEN STROGANOFF

SERVES 4

Cooking time: 6 to 8 hours on low

Creamy, delicious stroganoff is always a hit. Here I try to lighten it up a bit by using chicken instead of beef. The combination of cream cheese and sour cream make for a very authentic dish. If you're going to want to eat the moment you get home, you can cook noodles ahead of time and warm them in the microwave before serving.

2 pounds chicken breast, diced

1 cup chopped onion

8 ounces fresh mushrooms, sliced

1 can (10 ounces) cream of mushroom soup

½ packet French onion soup mix

3 teaspoons garlic, crushed or finely chopped

1 chicken stock cube

½ to ¾ cup warm water

¼ cup cream cheese

¼ cup sour cream

1 Put diced chicken breast in slow cooker. Top with onion and mushrooms.

2 In a separate bowl, combine remaining ingredients, except for the cream cheese and sour cream.

3 Pour soup mixture on top of chicken and vegetables. Stir.

4 Cover and cook on low for 6 to 8 hours.

5 In the last 15 minutes of cooking, add the cream cheese and sour cream; stir well to combine.

6 Serve over noodles.

 Note: When you add the sour cream, feel free to throw in any cooked vegetables you have on hand. Snow peas add a nice crunch.

CHICKEN & NOODLES

MAKES 4 SERVINGS

Cooking time: 1 hour on high, 5 to 6 hours on low, and about ½ hour on high

I just love this recipe. It's warm, comforting, and totally delicious. It makes me nostalgic for my mom's cooking. It was given to me by one of my favorite people and bloggers, Krista Marshall from *Everyday Mom's Meals*. Both of us have pretty much the same outlook on food—keep it tasty, but keep it simple too. About 1,500 miles separate us, and Krista and I often kid that the distance keeps us safe because we'd just raise too much heck together. But I still wish I was closer so I could sit at her table on a cold snowy night and enjoy a nice big bowl of this with her!

Olive oil
2½ pounds chicken tenders
Salt and pepper to taste
2 cups chicken broth
1 can (10.75 ounces) cream of chicken soup
1 medium white onion, diced
3 ribs celery, diced
3 carrots, diced
¾ cup frozen peas
1 bag (24 ounces) frozen egg noodles

1 Preheat oven to 375 degrees.

2 Drizzle olive oil over chicken and season with salt and pepper. Place chicken on baking sheet and roast for 30 minutes or until juices run clear.

3 Shred chicken with two forks or using stand mixer. Transfer chicken to slow cooker, and add chicken broth, soup, onion, celery, carrots, and peas. Season with salt and pepper. Stir to combine.

4 Cook on high for 1 hour. Reduce heat to low and cook an additional 5 to 6 hours.

5 Increase heat back to high and add frozen noodles. Allow to cook just until noodles are done, about 30 minutes. Do not overcook, or noodles will be mushy.

 Recipe courtesy of www.everydaymomsmeals.blogspot.com

CHICKEN *with* CREAMY MUSHROOM RICE

SERVES 4

Cooking time: 3 to 4 hours on high

This recipe was the test run for my then-brand-new casserole crock pot. It's been a big hit with anyone who's tried it. You can leave out the chicken and just make the rice as a special side dish, and you can use brown or regular rice if you want, but the jasmine has a particular flavor, so you won't get quite the same result. Many of my site readers have and pronounced the rice a "keeper." I can't disagree!

1 teaspoon oil for browning
8 chicken drumsticks (see Note)
2 cans (4 ounces each) sliced mushrooms, drained
2 tablespoons onion, minced
1 garlic clove, minced
1 can (10.25 ounces) cream of mushroom soup
2 cups milk
2 teaspoons salt
1 teaspoon pepper
¼ cup grated Romano or Parmesan cheese
¾ cup jasmine rice (or regular rice)

1   Heat oil in large skillet over medium-high heat. Brown chicken drumsticks on all sides; remove to a platter.

2   In the same skillet, brown the mushrooms, onions, and garlic. Remove from heat and add the soup. Slowly stir in milk. Add the salt, pepper, and cheese. Stir in the rice.

3   Transfer the soup and rice mixture to a 5- to 6-quart slow cooker (I used a casserole crock shaped like a 13 x 9-inch baker). Place drumsticks on top of rice (I could do this in a single layer with the rectangular cooker, but you may have to layer depending on the shape of your slow cooker).

4   Cook on high for 3 to 4 hours, or until chicken is done and rice is tender yet creamy.

 Note: You may use boneless, skinless breasts (I don't recommend it, as breast meat has a tendency to dry out with slow cooking), but if you do, use about 2 pounds.

CHICKEN *with* VEGETABLES

MAKES 4 SERVINGS

Cooking time: 6 to 8 hours on low or 5 to 6 hours on high

A popular slow-cooker recipe for chicken with vegetables calls for boneless, skinless breasts and Italian dressing. My sister, the real crock pot maven in our family, was visiting from England recently and suggested we try it with thighs and a "Mississippi-style" seasoning. That seemed more to our taste, since both of us prefer thighs to breasts for slow cooking. My sister is big on substituting in her recipes, and being as she's our family's expert, I never question her judgment—she's usually right (she was in this case), and she is my big sister after all!

4 large chicken thighs (or small chicken leg quarters)
1 pound fresh whole green beans (cut off stems)
4 medium red potatoes, cut in chunks
1 envelope chicken gravy mix
¼ cup ranch-dressing seasoning mix (recipe follows)
4 tablespoons (½ stick) unsalted butter
⅓ cup water

1 Place chicken pieces in center of a large (6+ quart) crockpot (an oval crock pot is best here if you have one).

2 Place green beans on one side of the chicken, and potatoes on the other side of the chicken.

3 In a small bowl, combine gravy mix and ranch-dressing seasoning mix. Sprinkle seasoning evenly over the chicken pieces only; top with the butter.

4 Pour half the water over the potatoes and the remaining half over the green beans.

5 Cover and cook on low for 6 to 8 hours, or on high 5 to 6 hours.

RANCH SEASONING MIX

I've taken to making my own ranch-dressing seasoning mix because I find that most store-bought mix combinations contain way too much salt. Here's the one I use now; double the amount of salt if you prefer. If you don't have time to make this, use the ready-made kind.

¾ cups dehydrated buttermilk powder or nonfat dry milk
½ cup dehydrated onions
¼ cup parsley
½ tablespoon salt
½ tablespoon garlic powder
½ teaspoon onion powder
½ teaspoon pepper

Mix all ingredients in a small bowl, then transfer to a covered container to store. Two tablespoons of this mixture is equal to one package of ranch-seasoning dressing mix.

FRUITY BBQ CHICKEN

MAKES 4 TO 6 SERVINGS

Cooking time: 4 hours on high or 8 hours on low

This recipe was one of my earliest ventures into what I like to call "experimental slow cooking." I wanted to see if I could, indeed, make crock-pot chicken taste like it came out of the oven or off the grill. The chicken is first roasted, without any liquid in the crock at all, then glazed later in the cooking process with the sauce. This is definitely not a set-and-forget type of recipe, but it's well worth the added effort!

3 pounds assorted chicken drumsticks and thighs
1 tablespoon salt
1 teaspoon pepper
1 teaspoon garlic powder
1 cup high-quality barbecue sauce (like Sweet Baby Ray's)
½ cup apricot or peach preserves (see Note)
2 teaspoons Dijon mustard

1 Remove skin from chicken if desired. Mix salt, pepper, and garlic powder and sprinkle over chicken; rub in well. Place chicken in the bottom of a 6- or 7-quart slow cooker (use an oval cooker if you have one), preferably in a single layer.

2 Cover and cook on high for 3 hours or on low for 6 hours (I recommend cooking on high). In a small bowl, mix barbecue sauce, preserves, and mustard. Set aside.

3 Remove chicken from slow cooker and place on a plate. Drain juices from the slow cooker crock and wipe the crock dry with a paper towel. Place chicken back in the slow cooker. Pour half the sauce mixture over the chicken. Cover and continue cooking on high for an additional 1 hour or low 2 hours.

4 Remove chicken from slow cooker and brush with more sauce (I reserve about ¼ to ½ cup for dipping, but you can use it all at this point if you wish). Put the chicken under the broiler for a minute or two to crisp it a bit if desired.

 Note: Concord grape jelly would probably be just as good.

TERIYAKI CHICKEN

SERVES 4 TO 6

Cooking time: 4 to 5 hours on high

My mom was forever sending away for recipe pamphlets from major brands. One of those pamphlets was from a big-brand soy sauce company and included a chicken dish I've never forgotten. The rest of the family didn't care for it, though, so she only made it one time. After Mom moved back to England, I got all her cookbooks and the zillion pamphlets, but the soy sauce one wasn't among them. I think it was teriyaki chicken, but I was so little at the time, I can't be sure. All I remember is the soy sauce! When I made this dish, I wasn't thinking about re-creating the earlier recipe, but the minute I tasted it, it reminded me of that childhood favorite. The slow cooker infuses the meat with a wonderful teriyaki flavor, right down to the bone.

1 tablespoon oil
2 pounds chicken thighs (may use skinless)
2 garlic cloves, minced
1 tablespoon grated fresh ginger or ½ teaspoon ground dry ginger
¼ cup water, plus another ¼ cup for thickening sauce
⅓ cup soy sauce
3 tablespoons honey
2 tablespoons molasses
1 tablespoon rice vinegar
¼ cup sherry (apple juice may be substituted)
4 green onions, sliced
½ teaspoon dark sesame oil
2 tablespoons cornstarch for thickening sauce
Green onions, sliced, for garnishing

1 Spray or line (with a slow cooker bag) a 5- to 6-quart slow cooker.

2 In a large heavy skillet, heat the oil and brown chicken very well on both sides. Place chicken in slow cooker.

3 Sauté garlic and ginger in the browning pan for about 1 minute. Add water, scraping up all the browned bits at the bottom of the pan. Add soy sauce, honey, molasses, vinegar, and sherry. Stir well and pour over chicken in slow cooker.

4 Cover slow cooker and cook on high for 4 to 5 hours (or until chicken is done). Remove chicken from the slow cooker and place on broiler pan. Set aside.

5 Add the sesame oil to the remaining slow cooker juices. (Note: If you used skin-on chicken you may want to transfer juice to a saucepan to skim off fat before thickening sauce.) Mix cornstarch with ¼ cup water. With slow cooker set to high, slowly add cornstarch mixture and stir until sauce is thickened. Let bubble about 1 minute to swell and cook the cornstarch.

6 Preheat broiler to high. Broil chicken about 3 minutes each side or until chicken surface is slightly caramelized and bubbly.

7 Place chicken on serving tray and pour sauce over chicken. Garnish with sliced green onions.

8 Jasmine rice makes a perfect accompaniment to this meal.

PORK

JUICY MAPLE PORK *with* SWEET POTATOES

SERVES 4 TO 6

Cooking time: 4 to 4½ hours on high

Another of my family's favorite fall meals. You can use either boneless or bone-in country-style pork ribs, but boneless is preferred. This is a well-balanced meal in terms of color—the caramel color of the pork, the white of the regular potatoes, and the deep orange of the sweets. All flavored with maple syrup. You can't go wrong with this one!

2 pounds country-style pork ribs (boneless preferred)
1 recipe Maple and Sage Seasoning Rub (recipe follows), divided
3 large white potatoes, peeled and cut in chunks
1 large sweet potato, peeled and cut in chunks
½ cup maple syrup

1 Cut pork into serving-sized portions. Rub with about ½ of the maple and sage seasoning. Place in a single layer in the bottom of the slow cooker.

2 Top with the potatoes and sprinkle about 2 tablespoons of the rub over the potatoes. Cover and set cooker to high. After about 2 hours, remove any accumulated fat/juice/liquid.

3 Return meat and potatoes to cooker and continue cooking on high for 1½ to 2 hours. Drizzle maple syrup over the pork and potatoes. Cook for an additional 30 minutes.

MAPLE & SAGE SEASONING RUB

MAKES ABOUT ¾ CUP

I modeled this on Taste of Inspirations Maple & Sage Pork Rub. Recipes calling for the homemade version can substitute with store-bought.

½ cup brown sugar
1 teaspoon ground sage
1 teaspoon ground thyme
1 teaspoon salt
½ teaspoon pepper
½ teaspoon ground ginger
½ teaspoon garlic powder
½ teaspoon maple extract
Pinch of nutmeg

In a small bowl, combine all ingredients and mix well. Store in an air-tight container.

APPLE BUTTER BBQ RIBS

MAKES 4–6 SERVINGS

Cooking time: 3½ to 5½ hours on high

Here's a delicious barbecue rib recipe adapted for the slow cooker. I served these ribs when my picky nephew, an excellent cook himself, was here on a visit from England. He absolutely loved them, and took the recipe home with him, although he had to make his own apple butter because he couldn't find it in the UK. He now uses the seasoning rub in many other recipes.

1 slab (about 3 to 4 pounds) pork baby back ribs

FOR THE MEAT SEASONING RUB
½ cup brown sugar
1 tablespoon garlic powder
2 teaspoons onion powder
½ teaspoon thyme
½ teaspoon salt
¼ teaspoon pepper
⅛ teaspoon cayenne pepper, optional

FOR THE SAUCE
½ cup good barbecue sauce (like Sweet Baby Ray's)
¼ cup apple butter

1 Prepare ribs by removing membrane covering the bone (silver skin), as this prevents the ribs from curling as they cook.

2 Mix rub ingredients together in a small bowl. Rub all sides of the ribs with prepared rub.

3 Place ribs in a large plastic ziplock bag and refrigerate overnight.

4 In a small bowl, mix together barbecue sauce and apple butter and set aside.

5 Cut ribs in 2-rib portions to fit inside the crock. Cover and cook on high for 3 to 5 hours (or until ribs are 170 degrees).

6 Remove ribs and drain off any accumulated liquid in the crock. Wipe the crock dry with paper towels.

7 Place ribs back in crock and pour desired amount of sauce over ribs—I suggest no more than ½ cup, as you want the flavor of the rub to come through and not be over-shadowed by the strength of the sauce. Cover and cook on high about 30 minutes or until glazed.

BROWN SUGAR COUNTRY-STYLE PORK RIBS

SERVES 4

Cooking time: 5 to 6 hours on low or 3 to 4 hours on high

Tender and inexpensive pork ribs cook to succulent perfection in a sweet yet tangy sauce right in your slow cooker. The flavor is even more intense if you thicken the sauce into a gravy and serve it over the top of the ribs. This recipe would definitely work with any style chops as well. With thicker chops (over $\frac{1}{2}$ inch thick) the cook times would be about the same as for the ribs; shorten the cook time for thinly sliced chops.

 Note: Country-style ribs are a well-marbled cut of pork. To reduce fat, make this a day ahead of time, refrigerate overnight, and skim off any congealed fat before reheating.

2 to 3 pounds country-style pork ribs
Oil for browning
1 teaspoon salt
½ teaspoon pepper
½ teaspoon garlic powder

FOR THE SAUCE
⅓ cup soy sauce
¾ cup pineapple juice or lemon-lime soda (like 7UP)
3 garlic cloves, crushed
½ cup brown sugar
2 tablespoons cornstarch, optional
¼ cup water, optional

1 Trim ribs of excess fat. Heat oil over medium-high heat in a heavy skillet.

2 Mix the salt, pepper, and garlic powder; sprinkle over pork. Brown pork well on both sides; place in crock of a 5- to 6-quart slow cooker.

3 Mix sauce ingredients in a small bowl and pour over pork. Cover and cook on low 5 to 6 hours, or high 3 to 4 hours. (Times are approximate.)

4 If a thick sauce is desired, remove ribs to a serving plate and keep warm in a 200 degree oven. Heat sauce on high setting until it begins to bubble. Mix in cornstarch and water, stirring constantly to avoid lumps. Cook for 5 minutes.

5 Return the ribs to the crock pot to coat with sauce, or ladle sauce over ribs on serving platter.

MISSISSIPPI RIBS

MAKES 4 TO 6 SERVINGS

Cooking time: 6 to 8 hours on low or 5 to 6 hours on high

This rib recipe is a takeoff of the famous Mississippi-style pot roast, and the flavor can't be beaten. If you're serving it to the kiddos, substitute apple juice for the whiskey and go easier on the hot sauce or eliminate it entirely.

4 to 5 pounds baby back or regular pork spare ribs
1 package au jus gravy mix
1 package dry ranch dressing mix
4 tablespoons butter, cut up
4 to 6 pepperoncini peppers

FOR THE GRAVY
2 tablespoon to ¼ cup Jack Daniel's whiskey
1 tablespoon hot sauce
3 tablespoons cornstarch
¼ cup water
1 teaspoon browning sauce (like Gravy Master or Kitchen Bouquet), optional, for color

1   Rinse ribs and cut into sections containing 2 to 3 ribs. Pat ribs dry and lay them on a baking sheet. Broil on high heat until ribs begin to brown. (You can eliminate this step, as it makes no difference to the taste; I find the browned ribs make for a better presentation.) Place ribs in a 5-quart or larger slow cooker.

2   Combine au jus and ranch dressing mixes in a small bowl.

3   Distribute butter pieces evenly over ribs, then sprinkle the mixed gravy/dressing mixture evenly over all. Lay the pepperoncini over the ribs.

4   Cover and cook on high for 5 to 6 hours or on low for 6 to 8 hours. (Times are approximate; mine were done in 5 hours on high.)

5   When ribs are done (the meat will easily fall off the bone, but ribs keep their shape when handled), remove them to a platter and cover to keep warm.

6   With slow cooker set to high setting, add the whiskey and hot sauce and stir.

7   Mix the cornstarch and water. While stirring liquid, pour in only enough of the cornstarch mixture to thicken gravy to your personal preference. Add browning sauce, if desired. Let the gravy cook about 5 minutes.

8   You may place the ribs back in the crock pot in the gravy to keep them warm if you're not eating immediately. Otherwise, pour the gravy in a gravy boat and serve it along with the ribs.

9   This is wonderful served with mashed potatoes.

CHEESE & POTATO STUFFED PORK CHOPS

SERVES 4

Cooking time: 4 to 5 hours on high

I got the idea for this from a good friend. I love Asiago cheese. Many of my recipes include it. Hers had the cheese only, but I wanted to create something around a stuffing reminiscent of scalloped potatoes, but one that had more of a kick. These certainly do. Just make sure to slice the potatoes tissue-paper-thin, otherwise they won't cook evenly.

4 center-cut bone-in pork chops (about ¾-inch thick)
2 medium potatoes (see Note)
½ cup shredded Fontina cheese
¼ cup shredded Asiago cheese
½ teaspoon salt
⅛ teaspoon pepper
3 tablespoons melted butter, divided

1 Using a sharp paring knife, make a "pocket" in the chops to hold the filling, a 2-inch incision from the outside edge of the chops all the way to the bone.

2 Peel the potatoes if desired. (I used white new potatoes so eliminated this step.) Slice the potatoes ultra thin . . . they should be so translucent you could read the newspaper through them. For this, I used my box grater—the side with the wide slots for slicing. Otherwise use a mandolin. Pat the potato slices between paper towels to remove excess moisture.

3 Place potatoes in a medium bowl. Add the cheeses, salt, pepper, and 1 tablespoon of the melted butter.

4 Stuff each chop with ¼ of the potato-cheese mixture. Place chops in a 5- to 7- quart slow cooker. Position chops with the stuffed pocket angled upward. Brush with remaining melted butter. Sprinkle lightly with additional salt and pepper.

5 Cover and cook on high for 4 to 5 hours.

 Note: Pre-frozen shredded potatoes (hash browns) may be substituted. Use about 2 cups, thawed.

CALYPSO PORK CHOPS

MAKES 6 SERVINGS

Cooking time: $6\frac{1}{4}$ to $8\frac{1}{4}$ hours on low

One day I found a couple of packages of vacuum-sealed pork chops in my freezer with popped seals. The chops weren't ruined but would be if I didn't use them promptly. I decided to make something with a highly flavored sauce just in case the meat had that "been in the freezer too long" taste. The chops were fine, and this great recipe was born. Perfect for a pork loin too!

Oil for browning
6 meaty bone-in pork chops
1 cup water, divided
1 can (20 ounces) pineapple chunks, undrained
¼ cup brown sugar
1 tablespoon soy sauce
1 tablespoon cider vinegar
2 teaspoons curry powder
½ teaspoon ground ginger
¼ to ½ teaspoon red pepper flakes
2 tablespoons cornstarch
2 green onions, sliced

1 Heat a heavy skillet over medium-high heat. Add oil. Brown pork chops well on all sides. Remove pork chops from pan. Deglaze pan with the ½ cup water, scraping up the browned bits. Reserve liquid and drippings.

2 In a medium bowl, combine pineapple, reserved liquid from the browning pan, brown sugar, soy sauce, vinegar, curry powder, ground ginger, and pepper flakes. Mix well and pour into the crock of a 5- to 7-quart slow cooker.

3 Place pork chops on top of sauce. Cook on low for 6 to 8 hours or until pork chops are tender.

4 Remove pork chops to serving plate and cover with foil to keep warm, preferably in a warm oven.

5 Mix the cornstarch and the other ½ cup water. Add to juice in slow cooker, stirring while adding; stir well. Cover slow cooker and cook sauce for 15 minutes.

6 Ladle sauce over pork chops. Top with sliced green onion.

PORK CHOP STROGANOFF

SERVES 4

Cooking time: 6 to 8 hours on low

No matter how long I've been cooking, I am always amazed at how sometimes the fewest ingredients produce the tastiest and most gourmet-style food. This is one of those recipes. I had a freezer full of pork chops and decided to try something different from the usual "bread 'em and bake 'em." I love stroganoff-style dishes and since I had nothing to lose really except some pork chops my dog would have gladly eaten (the cat too most likely), I went ahead and created this dish. Needless to say, the dog and the cat got no pork chops—this tasted great, and it's a real keeper!

1 can (10.75 ounces) cream of mushroom soup
1 envelope pork gravy mix
8 ounces sliced mushrooms (I used baby bellas)
4 large bone-in rib pork chops
1 tablespoon butter
½ cup water
⅓ cup sour cream

1 Mix the soup and the gravy mix in a small bowl. Add to the slow cooker. Add mushrooms on top of soup mixture.

2 Brown pork chops in butter in a large skillet. Transfer to slow cooker after browning, laying them atop the mushrooms.

3 Add the ½ cup water to the browning pan and deglaze, scraping up all the browned bits from the skillet; pour liquid over pork chops in slow cooker.

4 Cover and cook on low 6 to 8 hours. Remove pork chops to serving platter. Add the sour cream to liquid in the slow cooker and mix until smooth. Serve sauce on top of chops.

PORK CHOPS

with GOLDEN RANCH GRAVY

MAKES 4 SERVINGS

Cooking time: 3 to 4 hours on high or 4 to 6 hours on low

Here's another one of those recipes that are short on ingredients but long on flavor. No surprise, then, that it has always been one of my most popular recipes!

1 tablespoon butter

4 center-cut rib pork chops (bone-in or boneless)

1 can (10.75 ounce) cream of chicken soup

2 tablespoons Ranch Seasoning Mix (recipe page 53) or 1 package store-bought

1 Melt butter in a large, heavy skillet over medium heat. Brown pork chops well on both sides. Remove chops from pan and place in slow cooker.

2 Add the soup and ranch dressing mix to the same pan the pork chops were browned in. Mix well and heat.

3 Pour soup mixture over pork chops in slow cooker. Cover and cook on high 3 to 4 hours or low 4 to 6 hours.

4 Serve over rice.

74

CHEESY SAUSAGE & TATERS

SERVES 4 TO 6
Cooking time: 4 to 6 hours on low

This recipe was given to me by a member of my Facebook crock pot group who knows my weakness for anything with smoked sausage or kielbasa. I happened to have Cheddar-smoked sausage on hand so that's what I used, and it is perfect in this dish. But watch this one carefully so as not to overcook.

1 package (14 to 16 ounces) Cheddar-smoked sausage or kielbasa
32-ounce bag frozen potato nuggets (like Tater Tots)
2 cups shredded sharp or extra-sharp Cheddar cheese
1 cup light cream, half-and-half, or whole milk

1 Cut sausage in ¼-inch slices; set aside.

2 Place half the potato nuggets in the bottom of a 5- to 6-quart slow cooker. Layer half the sausage slices on top of the potatoes. Layer half the cheese over the sausage slices. Repeat for another layer.

3 Pour cream over top, cover, and cook on low for 4 to 6 hours.

BEEF

CLASSIC POT ROAST

SERVES 4 TO 8, DEPENDING ON SIZE OF THE ROAST

Cooking time: 6 to 10 hours on low

When it comes to pot roast, I'm pretty particular about how it's flavored. I didn't care for my mother-in-law's pot roast and will go as far to say that I actually hated the one my mother made. Both these women were good cooks, so there was nothing wrong with either of their versions, it's just that I didn't like them. So I created my own classic version.

1 can (10.5 ounces) cream of mushroom soup
1 package (0.87 ounces) brown gravy mix (or 2 tablespoons)
1 tablespoon instant onion
1 cup sliced mushrooms (optional)
2 beef stock cubes
2 cloves garlic, crushed
1 cup water
1 small bay leaf, optional
3- to 5-pound beef roast (like bottom round or rump)

1 Mix all ingredients, except beef roast, in a small bowl. Set aside.

2 Place beef roast in the crock of a 5- to 6-quart slow cooker. Pour soup mixture over roast. Cover and cook on low 6 to 10 hours.

3 Gravy may be thickened with flour and water or cornstarch and water if desired.

CLASSIC POT ROAST WITH VEGGIES

SERVES ABOUT 4

Cooking time: 5 to 6 hours on high or 8 to 10 hours on low

This is my other go-to pot roast recipe. I use it if I don't want the hassle of preparing a separate vegetable and mashed potatoes. It's basically become my "company" pot roast because it requires minimal prep and cooks by itself with little intervention, so I can spend more time with my guests. I've lately taken to cooking this on the day before I have company, since the flavor actually improves, and the fat congeals when chilled for easy removal.

1 recipe Maple and Sage Seasoning Rub (page 61)
3- to 4-pound boneless chuck roast
¼ cup chopped onion
1 pound carrots
2 celery stalks
1 pound small red potatoes (about 2 inches in diameter)
1 cup water
2 beef stock cubes
¼ teaspoon browning sauce (like Gravy Master or Kitchen Bouquet), optional, for color
2 tablespoons cornstarch (for each cup of liquid), optional
2 tablespoons water (for each cup of liquid), optional

1 Spray or line the crock of a 5- to 7-quart slow cooker.

2 Sprinkle seasoning rub on all sides of the meat and rub in well. Place meat and onion in slow cooker.

3 Peel carrots and slice in half crosswise. Cut celery stalks in 1-inch chunks. Peel potatoes. Place them all in the slow cooker.

4 Add the water and stock cubes. Cover slow cooker and cook on high for 5 to 6 hours or on low for 8 to 10 hours. (Times are approximate.)

5 When roast is done, remove meat and vegetables. Skim the fat from the liquid. Add browning sauce at this point if desired.

6 To thicken pan juices, turn slow cooker to high and stir in 2 tablespoons cornstarch mixed with 2 tablespoons water for each cup of pan juices. Stir constantly until well mixed. Cook for 1 minute after juices begin to bubble.

Note: I like to make my pot roast a day in advance; chilling the liquid overnight allows for easy removal of the congealed fat. The taste also improves when it sits overnight. Just store the meat and vegetables in a separate container from the pan juices. Skim the fat off the chilled pan juices and reheat the veggies and meat in a pan on the stove. When heated through, remove the meat and veggies and proceed with thickening the gravy, if desired, as above.

ROASTED BEEF

SERVES 6 TO 8

Cooking time: 5 hours on high or 8 hours on low

This divine slow-roasted beef comes from my friend Laureen King of *Art and the Kitchen*. Red wine, Guinness stout, and lovely herbs flavor the roast. Laureen has such an artistic touch with food; her presentations are simply gorgeous. But all of her recipes are tried-and-true dishes that she serves often to her family.

1 sirloin tip roast, 5 to 6 pounds
Salt and pepper
2 to 4 tablespoons olive oil
¼ cup flour
¾ cup red wine
3 tablespoons tomato paste
¾ cup Guinness beer
4 cups beef broth
1 tablespoon Worcestershire sauce
1 large onion, chopped
4 celery stalks, chopped
2 cups carrots, chopped
6 garlic cloves, chopped
3 to 4 sprigs fresh thyme
2 large bay leaves

1 Season roast with salt and pepper. In large skillet, heat 2 tablespoons olive oil and sear roast on all sides. Transfer to slow cooker.

2 In browning pan, add up to 2 more table-spoons of olive oil as necessary, then add flour and stir, cooking until browned.

3 Using a whisk, deglaze skillet with a couple of tablespoons of the red wine, then add tomato paste. After scraping all the brown bits from the pan, add the remaining wine, beer, beef broth, and Worcestershire sauce. Whisk broth to ensure no lumps. (Pour through strainer if necessary to remove any lumps). Set aside.

4 Add onion, celery, carrots, garlic, thyme, and bay leaves to crock pot, on top of roast.

5 Pour broth over roast and vegetables. Cover and cook until tender, approximately 5 hours on high, 8 hours on low.

Note: To thicken gravy to desired consistency, transfer broth to saucepan. Make a slurry: in a small jar, combine 1 tablespoon flour and ¼ cup of broth. Shake well. Heat broth on stove top to boiling, gradually adding flour mix while whisking; add a bit at a time until desired consistency is achieved. Reduce heat and cook for a few more minutes to thicken.

 Recipe courtesy of www.artandthekitchen.com

ASIAN BBQ BEEF STRIPS

MAKES 2 SERVINGS

Cooking time: 4 to 5 hours on high

I'm a big fan of Asian cuisine, so I'm always on the lookout for great Asian-inspired meals. I love to make barbecue beef tips as a sandwich filler, and this recipe adds an Asian flair. Originally I made this in my rice cooker, but then discovered that it works in the slow cooker just as well.

4 ounces lean sirloin steak, sliced very thin

¼ cup low-sodium soy sauce

2 tablespoons brown sugar

2 tablespoons dry sherry or dry white wine

1 tablespoon rice vinegar (white may be substituted)

1 teaspoon dark sesame oil

1 cup water

1 large garlic clove, crushed

1 slice fresh ginger or ¼ teaspoon ginger powder

2 tablespoons sesame teriyaki basting sauce or glaze (available in the Asian section of most groceries)

1 Place all ingredients, except the teriyaki glaze, in a 3-quart slow cooker, and stir to combine. Cook on high for 4 to 5 hours.

2 Remove beef tips from the cooker and drain. Toss with the teriyaki glaze. Serve on hard rolls or with rice or pasta and a salad.

BRAISED SHORT RIBS

SERVES 4 (2 RIBS EACH)

Cooking time: 4 to 6 hours on high or 8 to 10 hours on low

For years I tried to duplicate a short rib dish my late husband once ordered in a restaurant. He was crazy about it, and when he offered me a taste, I was sorry I didn't order it too. With time and a little luck I finally got it right.

1 tablespoon olive oil

4 pounds (about 8 ribs) beef short ribs

Salt and pepper

1 medium onion, chopped

3 garlic cloves, minced

½ cup sliced fresh mushrooms

½ cup water

2 beef stock cubes or 1 tub Knorr concentrated beef stock

1 can (14.5 ounces) diced tomatoes, undrained

1 pound peeled baby carrots

1 small bay leaf

1 teaspoon dried thyme (or 3 fresh sprigs)

1 Heat olive oil in a large, heavy sauté pan or skillet over medium-high heat. Season ribs with salt and pepper to taste.

2 Brown short ribs on all sides. Place browned ribs in a 6- to 7-quart slow cooker.

3 In the same pan you browned the ribs in, add the onion, garlic, and mushrooms and sauté over medium-low heat until onion is slightly tender (about 3 to 5 minutes).

4 Deglaze the pan with the ½ cup water, scraping up the browned bits. Add stock, diced tomatoes (including liquid), carrots, bay leaf, and thyme. Mix well. Pour contents of pan over ribs in slow cooker.

5 Cover slow cooker and cook on high 4 to 6 hours, or low 8 to 10 hours. (Cooking times are guides only, as slow cookers do cook at different rates. Check for doneness at minimum times for each setting.)

6 Remove ribs to serving platter, cover with foil, and keep warm in a low oven (approximately 200 degrees).

7 Remove as much fat from the pan juices as possible. Transfer pan juices to a large skillet and reduce sauce 50 percent over medium-high heat. This will take about 5 minutes. (This step may be eliminated; reducing sauce yields a more intense flavor.)

8 Pour sauce over ribs on serving platter. Serve with rice or over mashed potatoes.

MAPLE-GLAZED SHORT RIBS

SERVES 4

Cooking time: 4 to 5 hours on high

Short ribs are made for slow cooking. This is one dish where you can truly set it and forget it. The ribs don't fall apart even after the long cook time. The key to them coming out perfectly is to drain off any accumulated fat from the crock.

8 meaty beef short ribs
3 tablespoons Maple Sage Seasoning Rub (see page 61)
½ cup maple syrup

1 Apply seasoning rub to each beef rib. Place ribs in a 5- to 7-quart slow cooker, preferably in a single layer.

2 Cook on high for 4 to 5 hours.

3 Preheat broiler. Transfer ribs to a broiler pan and glaze ribs with maple syrup. Put under broiler for about 3 minutes to crisp.

CREAM & ALE SHORT RIBS

SERVES ABOUT 4 PEOPLE

(I had 8 short ribs and allowed 2 meaty ribs per person)
Cooking time: 4 to 6 hours on high or 8 to 10 hours on low

Here's one of those recipes that just screams British Gastro Pub! I can imagine sitting in one of those fancy restaurants out in the English countryside and enjoying something just like this. These ribs are slow cooked in a mellow ale that infuses the meat with such great flavor. It's truly a dish fit for a king!

1 package au jus gravy mix
¼ cup flour
2 tablespoons brown sugar
½ teaspoon thyme
1 bottle (12 ounces) ale or beer
1 tablespoon oil, for browning
4 to 6 pounds meaty beef short ribs
1 small onion, sliced
1 garlic clove, minced
½ cup water
¼ cup heavy cream

1 Mix au jus gravy mix, flour, brown sugar, and thyme in a small bowl, making sure to smooth out any lumps in the brown sugar. Place into a 4- to 6-quart slow cooker (I used a 3.5-quart casserole crock.) Add the ale and stir well to combine.

2 Heat a heavy skillet over medium-high heat. Add the oil and brown short ribs on all sides. Remove to a plate.

3 In the browning pan, sauté the onion and garlic, stirring constantly, for 3 to 5 minutes—don't allow to burn.

4 Deglaze the pan with the ½ cup water; mix the onions and water into the au jus mixture in the slow cooker.

5 Place the short ribs in the slow cooker, cover, and cook on high 4 to 6 hours or low 8 to 10 hours (times are approximate).

6 Remove the ribs to a serving plate. Stir in the heavy cream, combining well. Pour gravy over short ribs.

FRUITED SHORT RIBS

SERVES 4 TO 8 DEPENDING ON INDIVIDUAL APPETITES

Cooking time: 4 to 6 hours on high or 6 to 8 hours on low

I often bring dinner to a friend of mine who works long hours; he loves beef ribs, but has to watch his salt intake. So I wanted to make a highly flavored dish that didn't rely on processed food, which is typically high in salt. I had oranges and dried cherries on hand and decided to experiment. Asian cuisine often relies on tasty fruit combinations, and these turned out great, with a wonderful depth of flavor.

1 tablespoon olive oil
4 pounds meaty beef short ribs (about 8)
Salt and pepper
1 cup orange juice
½ cup dried cherries
1 tablespoon grated orange zest
2 tablespoons cornstarch
¼ cup water

1 Heat olive oil in a large, heavy sauté pan or skillet over medium-high heat. Season ribs with salt and pepper to taste.

2 Brown short ribs on all sides. Place ribs in slow cooker.

3 Drain off fat from skillet. Add orange juice and deglaze the pan, scraping up the browned bits. Pour liquid over ribs in slow cooker. Add cherries and orange zest.

4 Cover and cook on low 6 to 8 hours, or high 4 to 6 hours. (Times are approximate.)

5 Remove ribs from slow cooker to serving plate.

6 Pour juice from slow cooker into a small saucepan; skim off the fat. (I usually put liquid in a small bowl and place it in the freezer for about an hour so the fat congeals and can be removed easily. I keep the ribs warm while I do this by placing them back in the slow cooker and setting to warm.)

7 Mix the cornstarch and water. Heat the pan juices until they bubble and then stir in cornstarch mixture. Cook 1 minute. Pour sauce over ribs on serving platter.

BEEF
STROGANOFF

MAKES 4 TO 8 SERVINGS (DEPENDING ON INDIVIDUAL APPETITES)
Cooking time: 4 to 5 hours on high or 6 to 8 hours on low

I love beef stroganoff, and there are slow-cooker recipes for it all over the place. Problem is, so many of those recipes rely on cream of *something* soup . . . often to the exclusion of the real deal, sour cream. This recipe aims to remedy that.

2 tablespoons olive oil

2 pounds lean boneless round or chuck, cut into ¼-inch strips

8 ounces fresh crimini or button mushrooms, sliced

1 medium onion, sliced

2 garlic cloves, minced

1 cup rich beef stock

1 teaspoon salt

½ teaspoon pepper

2 tablespoons brandy

1 cup sour cream

2 teaspoons Dijon mustard

½ teaspoon paprika

2 ounces cream cheese or Neufchâtel cheese, cut in chunks

2 tablespoons flour

1 Heat a heavy skillet over medium-high heat. Add the oil. When the oil begins to shimmer, add the meat and brown well on all sides. Remove browned meat from pan and add to a 5-quart slow cooker.

2 Add the mushrooms, onion, and garlic to the pan and sauté for about 2 minutes. Add the stock to the pan and deglaze (scrape up all the browned bits at the bottom of the pan and incorporate them into the stock). Add contents of pan to the slow cooker. Add the salt, pepper, and brandy. Stir.

3 Cover and cook on low for 6 to 8 hours or on high for 4 to 5 hours.

4 In a small bowl, combine sour cream, mustard, paprika, cream cheese, and flour and mix well. Add to the slow cooker and stir until cream cheese is blended in. Cover and cook on low an additional 15 minutes.

5 Serve over egg noodles.

BRAISED STEAK

SERVES 4

Cooking time: 3 to 4 hours on high or 5 to 6 hours on low

This is the type of meal I just love to prepare. There's virtually no fussing, other than browning the meat, which I insist on doing before slow cooking since it adds *so* much flavor. And deglazing the browning pan improves the flavor even more.

1 can (10.75 ounces) cream of mushroom soup (lower sodium preferred)
1 envelope au jus gravy mix
1 tablespoon dehydrated (instant) onion flakes
1 small bay leaf
2 tablespoons olive oil
1 pound blade steak (also called minute or chicken steak)
½ cup water

1 Mix the soup, au jus mix, and dehydrated onion in a medium bowl. Add bay leaf. Set aside.

2 Heat oil in a large skillet over medium-high heat. Brown steaks on each side. Place steaks in slow cooker.

3 Deglaze the skillet with the ½ cup of water, scraping up all the browned bits in the pan. Add this to the soup mixture and stir well to combine. Pour over the steaks in the slow cooker.

4 Cover and cook on high 3 to 4 hours or low 5 to 6 hours (times are approximate, as all slow cookers cook differently—mine was done at 3½ hours on high).

5 Remove the steaks to a serving platter. Stir gravy in the crock; remove bay leaf. Pour gravy over steaks.

GINGER BEEF
with MANDARIN ORANGES

MAKES 4 TO 6 SERVINGS
Cooking time: 4 to 5 hours on high or 8 to 10 hours on low

This has to be one of the best meals I have ever eaten, slow cooked or not. It is so full of flavor, and when paired with jasmine rice, it truly sings.

2 pounds boneless beef chuck roast

2 tablespoons vegetable oil, divided

1 cup thickly sliced mushrooms

1 can (8-ounces) sliced water chestnuts, drained

1 small onion, sliced

⅓ cup low-sodium soy sauce

1 tablespoon grated fresh ginger or 1 teaspoon ground ginger

1 tablespoon sherry or mirin

1 can (11-ounces) mandarin orange sections (reserve juice)

2 tablespoons cornstarch

1 cup beef stock

3 green onions, chopped

1. Trim beef of visible fat. Slice in ¼-inch slices. Line the crock of a 5-quart slow cooker with a cooking bag or spray with nonstick spray.

2. Heat 1 tablespoon of the oil in a large, heavy skillet over high heat. When oil just begins to smoke, add the beef slices, making sure not to overcrowd the pan (do this in two shifts if necessary). Brown well on both sides. Place browned beef in the slow cooker.

3. Heat the other 1 tablespoon of oil over medium-high heat. Add the mushrooms, water chestnuts, and onion. Sauté until onion begins to get soft. Add the soy sauce, ginger, and sherry, scraping up all the browned bits at the bottom of the pan. Place the mushroom mixture on top of the meat in the slow cooker.

4. Drain the mandarin orange slices. Set the drained sections aside. Combine reserved mandarin orange syrup and cornstarch and mix well. Add the beef stock to the orange/cornstarch mixture; stir well. Pour over meat and vegetables in the slow cooker.

5. Cover and cook on high 4 to 5 hours or on low for 8 to 10 hours. Mix in the reserved mandarin orange sections immediately before serving. Top with chopped green onion.

6. Serve over rice. Jasmine rice is especially good here.

CHOPPED STEAK with ONION MUSHROOM GRAVY

MAKES 2 TO 4 SERVINGS DEPENDING ON INDIVIDUAL APPETITES

Cooking time: 6 to 8 hours on low

This is another childhood-memory dish that I've adapted for the slow cooker. Chopped steak was one of my mom's go-to stovetop dinners because it was quick to make, inexpensive, and tasty. Sometimes she'd use cube steak instead of making ground beef patties, especially if they were on sale. So here's one family tradition I carried on in married life, because this became one of my late husband's favorites too. The recipe is very similar to Salisbury steak, but without all the fuss!

¼ cup plain bread crumbs

2 tablespoons instant minced onion

½ teaspoon garlic powder

2 low-sodium or regular beef stock cubes, crushed

¼ cup milk

1 pound very lean ground beef

1 tablespoon olive oil

¼ cup flour

1 can (10.75 ounces) low-sodium or regular cream of mushroom soup

1 can (10.75 ounces) condensed French onion soup

1 package brown gravy mix

1 cup sliced mushrooms

2 tablespoons water

1 In a medium bowl combine bread crumbs, onions, garlic powder, crushed stock cubes, and milk. Mix and let stand about 5 minutes.

2 Add ground beef to the bread crumb mixture and mix well. Form beef into 4 thin burgers. Heat a large skillet over high heat and add oil.

3 Dust burgers with flour, then add to hot skillet. Cook burgers for about 1 minute each side, just to brown.

4 Transfer burgers to slow cooker (I used a 5-quart), stacking if necessary.

5 Combine cream of mushroom soup, onion soup, gravy mix, and mushrooms in a small bowl. Pour soup mix over burgers.

6 Cover and cook on low 6 to 8 hours.

SWISS STEAK

MAKES 6 SMALL OR
3 LARGE SERVINGS

Cooking time: 4 to 5 hours on high or 6 to 8 hours on low

My main objection to most Swiss steak recipes is the inclusion of tomatoes. Not that I have anything against tomatoes—I love them, just not in this dish! Most recipes also call for round or thick-cut chuck roast. This recipe, however, uses blade steak. Yes, blade is chuck, the roundish cut of beef with the line of gristle through it that sits just below the blade bone. In some sections of the country, blade steak is known as chicken steak.

4 tablespoons olive oil, divided
8 ounces fresh mushrooms, thinly sliced
6 medium beef blade steaks (aka chicken steak)
Salt and pepper to taste
1 medium onion, sliced
1 tablespoon fresh thyme, minced
1½ teaspoons sweet paprika
¼ cup flour
¾ cup chicken stock
¼ cup dry sherry
½ cup heavy cream
2 tablespoons fresh parsley, chopped

1 Heat a heavy skillet or sauté pan over medium heat and add 1 tablespoon of the oil. Add the mushrooms and cover; cook 5 minutes. Remove cover and continue cooking until mushrooms begin to brown. Remove from pan and place in the slow cooker.

2 Return pan to the heat. Season the steaks with salt and pepper. Add 1 tablespoon of the oil and brown the blade steaks nicely. Remove to a plate and set aside.

3 Return pan to the heat and add 2 tablespoons of the oil. Add the onion, the thyme, and the paprika. Stir and cook for about 1 minute. Add the flour and stir well, cooking for about 1 minute. Whisk in the chicken stock and sherry, scraping up all the browned bits at the bottom of the pan. Add the entire contents of the pan to the slow cooker.

4 Place browned steaks on top of the mushroom and onion mixture in slow cooker. Cover and cook on low for 6 to 8 hours, or high for 4 to 5 hours.

5 Remove steaks to a serving plate and cover with aluminum foil to keep them warm. Stir the cream and parsley into the liquid in slow cooker. Heat for another 10 minutes. Ladle gravy over steaks and serve.

MISSISSIPPI SWISS STEAK

SERVES 6 TO 8

Cooking time: 3 to 5 hours on high or 4 to 6 hours on low

Based on the famous Mississippi-style pot roast, the secret to this tender Swiss steak is the cut of beef used—blade steak. Often called "chicken steak" or "minute steak," blade steak comes from the chuck area. Often overlooked because of its central strand of gristle, it's a tasty and versatile beef cut. It's actually the gristle that keeps it intact during long, slow cooking. The gristle is easily removed when served.

6 tablespoons unsalted butter
1 package au jus gravy mix
1 tablespoon Ranch Seasoning Mix (recipe page 53)
2 pounds blade steak or cube steak
¼ cup pepperoncini peppers

1 Cut butter into chunks. Mix the au jus gravy mix and the ranch dressing mix in a small bowl.

2 Place steaks in the crock of a 4- to 6-quart slow cooker (I used a casserole crock with an insert the size of a 13 x 9-inch baking dish).

3 Distribute butter pieces evenly over steaks, and sprinkle with the gravy and ranch seasoning mixture. Add the pepperoncini peppers.

4 Cover crock pot and set on high for 3 to 5 hours or low 4 to 6 hours. (Times will vary according to type of slow cooker used and how much the crock is filled—e.g., less than full will cook faster.)

5 At end of cooking time, remove steaks and stir gravy in crock until smooth. Pour gravy over steaks.

ORANGE BEEF WITH FIRE PEPPERS

MAKES 6 TO 8 SERVINGS

Cooking time: $3^1/_4$ to $5^1/_2$ hours on high

This dish has an absolutely wonderful flavor owing to the orange juice and zest, not to mention a colorful variety of bell peppers. The secret to keeping the peppers from getting mushy is to add them shortly before serving.

1 cup flour

1 teaspoon salt

½ teaspoon pepper

2 pounds beef round, shoulder, or sirloin, cut in ½-inch slices

1 cup orange juice

¾ tablespoon orange zest

3 tablespoons soy sauce

½ tablespoon dark sesame oil

2 tablespoons sugar

1 beef stock cube

2 tablespoons olive oil for browning

2 tablespoons minced garlic

8 ounces fresh mushrooms, sliced

1 medium onion, sliced

1 medium green bell pepper, cut in strips

1 medium yellow bell pepper, cut in strips

1 medium red bell pepper, cut in strips

2 to 3 tablespoons cornstarch, optional, for thickening sauce

4 to 5 tablespoons water, optional

1 Mix the flour, salt, and pepper and coat the meat with it.

2 Mix the orange juice, orange zest, soy sauce, sesame oil, sugar, and stock cube in a small bowl. (Double the amount of these ingredients if you prefer a saucier dish.) Set aside.

3 Heat a large, heavy skillet over medium-high heat. Add oil. Brown meat well. Add garlic. Add the orange juice mixture and deglaze pan, scraping up all the browned bits in the skillet. Add contents of skillet to slow cooker.

4 Cover slow cooker and set to high. Cook for about 3 to 4 hours.

5 Add the mushrooms, onion, and peppers. Cover and cook for an additional 15 to 30 minutes, depending on how crisp you like your bell peppers.

6 If you desire a thicker sauce, add the cornstarch and water mixture—just enough to reach desired thickness. Cook for an additional 1 to 2 minutes.

107

SICHUAN BEEF
WITH CARROTS

SERVES ABOUT 4

Cooking time: 3 to 5 hours on high or 5 to 7 hours on low

This is my version of the Chinese restaurant classic. Real beef with carrots is a stir-fry dish, but I wanted to see if I could make a stewed version of it. And this recipe doesn't disappoint. Chinese cuisine, no matter what the region, includes lots of stews. Sichuan Province is in the south of China, where it gets cold; the cuisine includes a number of stews containing hot peppers grown in the region. So while you sit back and relax, your slow cooker can whip up a little bit of China for the entire family!

1 cup carrots, cut lengthwise (approximately ¼-inch thick)
1 tablespoon olive oil, for browning meat
1½ pounds boneless chuck roast, cut in cubes
1½ cups water
2 garlic cloves, crushed
1 tablespoon brown sugar
½ teaspoon red pepper flakes
⅓ cup soy sauce (low-sodium if preferred)
2 tablespoon hoisin sauce
½ teaspoon dark sesame oil
1½ tablespoons cornstarch, optional, for thickening sauce
3 tablespoons water, optional
Small red chili peppers, optional, for garnishing
Sliced green onions, optional, for garnishing

1 Place carrots in the bottom of the crock pot.

2 Heat skillet over medium-high heat; add oil. When oil starts to shimmer, add meat and brown on all sides; remove meat from pan and place in the slow cooker on top of carrots. Add the 1½ cups water to the browning pan and deglaze, scraping up all the browned bits in the pan.

3 Add the garlic, brown sugar, red pepper flakes, soy sauce, hoisin sauce, and sesame oil. Stir thoroughly then pour contents of pan over the meat and carrots in the crock pot.

4 Cook on high 3 to 5 hours, or low 5 to 7 hours. (Times are approximate.)

5 *To thicken sauce, if desired*: When meat and carrots are done, remove from the slow cooker and keep warm. Turn slow cooker to high. Mix the cornstarch and water and stir into hot liquid, stirring until smooth. Cover and cook 15 minutes. Return the meat and carrots to the slow cooker. Heat through and serve. Top with red chili peppers and/or sliced green onions, if desired.

STUFFED BEEF ROLLS

MAKES 6 BEEF ROLLS

Cooking time: 3 to 4 hours on high or 6 to 8 hours on low

Anyone who knows German cuisine will recognize this immediately as a rouladen knockoff—and that's exactly what it is! I can't count how many times I made the real thing for my late husband. It was one of his favorite meals. This recipe replaces the usual onion and pickle with a soft breadcrumb stuffing, but the bacon remains. Bacon always must remain! Cube steaks work well here, because they are easy to stuff and roll and you don't have to pound them down like the more traditional round steaks. Why work harder than you have to?

¼ cup finely chopped onion

¼ cup finely chopped mushrooms, plus 2 cups thickly sliced mushrooms

¼ cup grated carrots

1 tablespoon butter

2 cups soft breadcrumbs

4 slices crisp-cooked bacon, diced

1 teaspoon salt

¼ teaspoon pepper

6 large beef round cube steaks (see Note)

2 packages brown gravy mix, prepared with 1 ¼ cups water (or 1 ½ cups gravy)

1¼ cups water

1 In a skillet over medium-low heat, sauté chopped onion, finely chopped mushrooms, and carrots in butter.

2 Combine breadcrumbs, bacon, salt, and pepper in a medium bowl. Add the sautéed vegetables, including the butter from the pan. Mix well.

3 Place about ¼ cup of stuffing on each cube steak and roll up from the narrow end, securing with a toothpick if desired. If there is stuffing left over, cover and set aside.

4 Place beef rolls in slow cooker, cover, and cook on high 3 to 4 hours, or low for 6 to 8 hours.

5 *If using gravy mix*: At the end of main cooking time, remove rolls from slow cooker and set aside. Combine gravy mix and water in a small bowl or measuring cup, and stir, making sure there are no lumps. Pour liquid into slow cooker set to high, and add the thickly sliced mushrooms. Stir until thickened. Return beef rolls to cooker, cover, and cook an additional 15 minutes.

6 *If using prepared gravy*: Pour gravy over beef rolls at end of main cooking time, cover the crock pot, and cook for an additional 15 minutes on high, or until gravy is heated. If there is reserved stuffing, reheat in a microwave on high and serve beef rolls over the stuffing.

 Note: Thin beef round steaks labeled "for braciole" can be substituted

MAPLE MEAT LOAF

SERVES 4 TO 6

Cooking time: 3 to 5 hours on high or 6 to 8 hours on low

1 cup dry poultry stuffing such as Pepperidge Farm
2 tablespoons finely chopped onion
2 tablespoons warm water
1 pound lean ground beef
8 ounces maple-flavored bulk sausage
2 large eggs

1 In a large bowl, combine stuffing mix and onion. Add the warm water and toss to coat. Crumbs should not be wet, just slightly damp. Let this stand until water is absorbed, 5 minutes or so.

2 Add remaining ingredients to bowl and mix well.

3 Shape into loaf and place in a 5-quart slow cooker (preferably on a rack) and cook on low for 6 to 8 hours, or high for 3 to 5 hours.

4 Slice and serve. Mashed potatoes and gravy are a nice accompaniment.

I wasn't always a fan of meatloaf. For years I tried recipe after recipe thinking maybe I'd hit on the right one. I'd read somewhere that adding bulk breakfast sausage adds a new dimension to this everyday meal, so I decided I'd try it. I had no breadcrumbs on hand, so I substituted some poultry stuffing mix. What I didn't realize until after the loaf was in the oven was that I'd used maple-flavored sausage instead of regular. Oops! I figured the dogs would have a good meal, but after it started cooking and the aroma from the oven hit me, I couldn't wait to try it. This is one terrific meatloaf . . . and all because of what I thought was a mistake. Here it is, adapted for the slow cooker.

CHILI HATER'S CHILI

SERVES ABOUT 6

Cooking time: 6 to 8 hours on low

When I was a young, I couldn't understand why I didn't like chili. It's such a popular dish; who doesn't like chili? I didn't! Years later I discovered the reason—cumin. My native Texan friend Babs always calls me on the carpet for dissing this spice, and even tells me her house is infused with the scent. But that aside, I hit on a very nice, yet authentic, spice blend (no cumin!) that turned me into a chili lover.

1 pound lean ground beef, browned and drained
½ cup chopped onion
3 large garlic cloves, minced
1 can (about 16 ounces) dark red kidney beans, drained and rinsed
1 can (about 16 ounces) garbanzo beans (chickpeas), drained and rinsed
1 (15-ounce) can tomato sauce
1 (10 ounce) can chopped tomatoes and green chiles (like Rotel)
½ cup chopped green bell pepper
½ cup chopped red bell pepper
1 to 2 long, dried chile peppers
2 teaspoons chili powder
1 teaspoon dry mustard
½ teaspoon dried basil
¼ teaspoon ground black pepper

1 Place ground beef, onion, and garlic in a skillet over medium-high heat and cook until meat is browned and onion is translucent; drain and add to slow cooker.

2 Add remaining ingredients to slow cooker, stir to mix, and cover and cook on low 6 to 8 hours.

3 Serve with rice and top with shredded sharp Cheddar cheese.

PASTA

BAKED ZITI

MAKES 6 SERVINGS

Cooking time: 4 to 6 hours on low

This wonderful recipe is from my friend Vonnie who blogs at *My Catholic Kitchen*. It's one of her favorite things to make for her family, and they just gobble it up. And there's good reason for that—it's totally delicious. This started out being a meatless meal, but Vonnie has made it with meat and says it's equally as good as the meatless version. She finds this recipe a godsend on those days where she really can't devote much time to meal preparation because of chores and other family obligations. Try this—and you'll see why it's gone viral several times!

1 container (15 ounces) ricotta cheese

1 egg

½ teaspoon Italian seasonings

1 bag (16 ounces) shredded Italian cheese blend, (divided)

1 cup water

2 jars (24 ounces each) pasta sauce

1 pound dry ziti pasta

1 Coat the inside of slow cooker with cooking spray.

2 In bowl, combine ricotta, egg, Italian seasonings, and ½ the bag of cheese. Set aside.

3 In a large bowl, combine water, 1 jar of sauce, and pasta. Put ¼ of the pasta in the bottom of the slow cooker. Layer half the ricotta mixture over the pasta, dropping by the spoonful and then using the back of spoon to smooth into an even layer. Top with half the remaining jar of sauce and then the other half of ricotta mixture. Put the rest of the pasta on top. Pour the remaining sauce over that. Use the remaining cheese to sprinkle over the top.

4 Cook on low heat for 4 to 6 hours.

5 Serve directly from slow cooker.

  Note: For a meat option, add ½ pound cooked ground meat and ½ pound cooked Italian sausage into the sauce before layering.

  Recipe courtesy of www.mycatholickitchen.com

FIVE-CHEESE LASAGNA

SERVES ABOUT 6

Cooking time: 3 to 5 hours on high or 4 to 6 hours on low

The slow cooker is the perfect vessel for lasagna, one of the most popular casseroles ever. Slow cooking makes for a very flavorful lasagna. When I was growing up, my mom made a pretty much standard version of this—in the oven, of course. I'm now a bit more adventurous in my tastes and this lasagna pretty much illustrates that. My belief is the more cheese the better, and I do appreciate a bit of heat (you can easily adapt this for something with less of a bite if preferred). Another wonderful benefit of using your slow cooker for pasta of any kind: you don't have to precook it!

1 pound hot Italian sausage

1 cup ricotta cheese

¼ cup grated Romano or Parmesan cheese

3 to 4 pepperoncini peppers, diced, optional

1 teaspoon hot red pepper flakes

1 pound lean ground beef

1 jar (24 ounces) pasta sauce

1 cup water

9 lasagna noodles, uncooked (approximately)

½ cup shredded aged Asiago cheese

1 cup cubed fresh Asiago cheese, or mozzarella

1 pound mozzarella, sliced (reserve a few slices for top)

1 Cut sausage into ½-inch pieces. Mix the ricotta cheese with the grated Romano or Parmesan, the pepperoncini, if using, and the hot pepper flakes. Set aside.

2 In a large skillet, brown the sausage and ground beef. Drain off fat. Remove from heat.

3 Add the pasta sauce and water to the pan with the meat. Stir, combining well.

4 Place 1 cup of meat sauce in the bottom of a 3½- to 6-quart slow cooker. Layer noodles over the sauce, breaking noodles if necessary to fit. Distribute ½ of the ricotta mixture evenly across noodles. Distribute ½ of the other cheeses evenly, but hold back a few slices of mozzarella for the final topping. Top with about 1 cup of sauce. Repeat, ending with a layer of noodles. Top with remaining sauce.

5 Cover and set slow cooker on high for 3 to 5 hours, or low for 4 to 6 hours.

6 Place reserved mozzarella on top of lasagna. Place lid back on crock and let cheese melt. Turn off crockpot and let lasagna stand for about 10 to 15 minutes before slicing.

SPAGHETTI & MEAT SAUCE

SERVES 8

Cooking time: at least 2 hours on low

Here is another family favorite courtesy of Laureen King from *Art and the Kitchen*. I've made slow-cooker spaghetti sauce, but my recipe isn't half as good as hers, so that's why I'm sharing it with all of you! This is absolutely delicious and takes spaghetti from humdrum to fabulous.

2 pounds extra-lean ground beef

1 onion, chopped

4 garlic cloves, minced

2 small cans tomato sauce

2 small cans tomato paste

1 can tomato soup

½ to 1 cup water

1½ teaspoon basil

1½ teaspoon oregano

1 teaspoon thyme

3 small bay leaves

1 teaspoon salt (I usually use kosher salt)

1 teaspoon fresh ground pepper

½ cup Parmesan cheese

2 tablespoons butter

1. Brown ground beef and transfer to a heated crockpot. Using the same pan, sauté onion until almost translucent. Add garlic and sauté another 2 minutes. (Don't burn the garlic or sauce will be bitter.)

2. Add the tomato sauce to deglaze the pan, scraping up any browned bits. Add tomato paste, tomato soup, and ½ cup water and stir, adding up to another ½ cup water until preferred consistency is achieved. Add basil, oregano, thyme, bay leaves, salt, and pepper and cook, stirring, until sauce is heated.

3. Pour sauce over ground beef in crock pot and stir well to combine.

4. Cook on low setting for at least 2 hours. (I usually let sauce cook all afternoon until ready to serve.) Add Parmesan cheese and butter in about the last hour of cooking.

5. Serve over spaghetti.

 Recipe courtesy of www.artandthekitchen.com

CREAMY PENNE

SERVES 4 TO 6

Cooking time: 2 to 3 hours on high

This is the ultimate comfort meal. It's cheesy and meaty. You can make it with ground beef or sausage, but either way, it's just a perfect family-style meal. Dress it up a bit by adding some vodka for an adults-only dish!

1 pound lean ground beef or bulk pork sausage

1 small onion, chopped

½ cup sliced mushrooms

1 teaspoon garlic powder

1 teaspoon salt

½ teaspoon pepper

1 can (15 ounces) diced tomatoes, undrained

1 box (16 ounces) dry penne pasta (or similar shape)

¼ cup grated Parmesan or Romano cheese

½ cup grape tomatoes

8 ounces cream cheese, cubed

¼ cup vodka, optional

1 to 2 cups water (see Note)

1 to 2 jars (26 ounces each) pasta sauce

1 Brown the ground beef (or bulk sausage), onion, and mushrooms in a large skillet. Season with garlic powder, salt, and pepper. Drain any excess fat. Set aside.

2 Pour diced tomatoes, including the juice, into a 5- by 7-quart slow cooker. Layer uncooked pasta on top of tomatoes.

3 Top pasta with beef mixture, grated cheese, and grape tomatoes. Place cubed cream cheese on top of the meat and tomato layer.

4 Add vodka, if using, 1 cup of water, and 1 jar of the pasta sauce.

5 Cook on high for 2 to 3 hours; stir and test pasta for doneness. Add the extra jar of pasta sauce and more water, if desired, to achieve preferred consistency. Cover and continue to cook on high for an additional 30 minutes or until heated through and pasta is desired doneness.

Note: The measurement range for water and pasta sauce reflects the fact that slow cookers vary in how they cook. If you prefer more sauce, you may want to add more liquid. For this dish, I used 1 jar of sauce and 1 cup of water. Start out with that ratio. You can add additional sauce and/or water when cooking is almost finished.

SIDES

CANDIED ACORN SQUASH

MAKES 4 SERVINGS

Cooking time: 2 to 3 hours on high or 4 to 6 hours on low

This was always a treat at our Thanksgiving dinner. Mom would often serve them halved, right out of the oven, but sometimes she would mash them; they're delicious either way! When acorn squash are in season, I've taken to making them the main part of everyday meals. They're a great addition to a meatless-meal rotation.

2 acorn squash, cut in half lengthwise and seeded
4 tablespoons brown sugar, divided
2 tablespoons butter, divided
½ cup water

1 Place squash halves rind side down in a large (5- to 6-quart) slow cooker. Fill each seed cavity with 1 tablespoon of the brown sugar and ½ tablespoon of the butter. Pour water around the squash.

2 Cook on low 4 to 6 hours, or high 2 to 3 hours.

CANDIED BABY CARROTS

MAKES 4 TO 6 SERVINGS

Cooking time: 2 to 4 hours on high or 4 to 6 hours on low

I just love these carrots. My mom used to make them on the stovetop, but they are perfect for the slow cooker as well. They pair nicely with pork and chicken and also make a great side at Thanksgiving for those who aren't crazy about sweet potatoes. I start with the ready-to-cook bags you buy in the produce section because it eliminates peeling and cutting, but if you don't mind the extra steps and don't want the added expense of the bagged variety, then use regular carrots.

2 pounds peeled baby carrots
½ teaspoon ground cinnamon
1 cup dark brown sugar
4 tablespoons (½ a stick) unsalted butter, cut up
½ cup water

1 Place carrots in a 4- to 6-quart lightly greased slow cooker. Mix cinnamon and brown sugar; distribute evenly over carrots. Distribute butter pieces evenly over top of carrots and add water.

2 Cook on low for 4 to 6 hours, or high 2 to 4 hours.

CITRUS GREEK POTATOES

MAKES 4 TO 6 SERVINGS
Cooking time: 5 hours on high

Direct from sunny Greece, my friend Katerina Delidimou brings you a favorite side of hers, adapted for the slow cooker. I love this authentic dish because it reminds me of warm, inviting Grecian climes!

2 garlic cloves, cut in two
8 medium potatoes, cut in four lengthwise
1 onion, sliced
Salt and pepper
½ cup olive oil
½ cup orange juice
1 tablespoon honey
1 teaspoon dried basil
2 teaspoons dried oregano
½ teaspoon dried thyme
1 teaspoon paprika
2 tablespoons orange marmalade

1 Scatter the garlic pieces in the crock of a slow cooker and top with the potatoes. Add the onion slices. Season with salt and pepper.

2 In a glass bowl combine oil, orange juice, honey, basil, oregano, thyme, and paprika and mix well. Pour liquid over potatoes, and scatter the marmalade on top.

3 Cook on high for about 5 hours. Just before the end of the cooking time, fire up your broiler. Place potatoes in an oven-safe Pyrex bowl or pan just until they take on a nice color, about 3 minutes. Monitor potatoes carefully while they're under the broiler to avoid burning. Remove, let them rest for 5 minutes, and serve.

 Recipe courtesy of www.culinaryflavors.gr

HOT GERMAN POTATO SALAD

MAKES 4 TO 6 SERVINGS

Cooking time: 5½ to 6½ hours on low

I'll never forget the first time I ate this. I was 18 and at a German festival in New Jersey with my bestie, her aunt, and her aunt's new husband (who was German). Bill went to get all of us food, which included brats, sauerkraut, beer, and this strange substance he called "potato salad." Being a thoroughly American kid despite being raised by a British mother, what I called potato salad was a mayonnaisy concoction that was served cold. This one was warm, and frankly, I didn't like it at all. But over the years, tastes do change and I became more sophisticated in my food choices . . . and marrying a German was a help!

1½ pounds small red potatoes
1 small onion, chopped
¾ cup water
4 slices bacon
¼ cup plus 2 tablespoons cider vinegar
2 tablespoons sugar
½ teaspoon celery seed
1 teaspoon salt
¼ teaspoon pepper
2 tablespoons flour

1 Scrub the potatoes and cut in ¼-inch slices.

2 Layer half the potatoes and half the onion in a small (3- to 4-quart) slow cooker. Repeat with remaining potatoes and onion. Pour water over potatoes and onion. Cook on low 5 to 6 hours.

3 Using a slotted spoon, transfer potatoes and onions to a plate. Set aside.

4 Slice bacon in 1-inch pieces. In a large (10 x 12-inch) skillet, cook bacon pieces until crisp. Remove from pan with slotted spoon and drain on paper towels.

5 Mix the vinegar, sugar, celery seed, salt, pepper, and flour, stirring so there are no lumps. Add vinegar mixture to crock pot and stir until liquid thickens slightly. Let cook on high for 5 minutes. Add the potatoes back to the crock pot along with the bacon, and stir gently to combine.

6 Turn to low and cook an additional 30 minutes.

CHEESY HASHBROWN CASSEROLE

SERVES 6

Cooking time: 1½ hours on high and 2½ hours on low

This is my version of the famous Cracker Barrel recipe. It's a side dish that can serve as a meal in itself. I often add some cooked breakfast sausage to it for a bit more oomph, but it's equally as good meatless! Such a versatile dish.

2 cans (10.75 ounces each) cream of chicken soup
1 cup sour cream or Greek yogurt
1 cup shredded Monterey Jack cheese
1 cup shredded Cheddar cheese
¼ cup finely chopped onion
1 teaspoon salt
½ teaspoon pepper
¼ cup butter, melted
8 ounces cooked breakfast sausage sliced in ½-inch
    pieces, optional
1 bag (30 ounces) shredded hashbrown potatoes, thawed
    (the plain kind)

1 Spray or grease the crock of a 5-quart (or larger) slow cooker, or use a liner.

2 In a large bowl, mix everything but the shredded potatoes.

3 Gently fold in the shredded potatoes.

4 Add the potato mixture to the slow cooker and spread out into an even layer.

5 Cook on high 1 hour 30 minutes, then turn to low and cook an additional 2 hours 30 minutes.

SPICY ROASTED CHILI CHEESE FRIES

MAKES 4 SERVINGS

Cooking time: 4 hours on high or 8 hours on low

Here's another distinctive and throughly delicious slow-cooker side dish from my friend Lisa Summers, aka the Creole Contessa. I'm always telling her that it's pretty lucky we live on opposite coasts, because if I were closer, I would not be able to stop myself from overindulging on her to-die-for creations. This recipe brings on the heat, so if you're a bit wimpy about hot stuff, feel free to adjust the seasonings.

4 tablespoons plus 1 teaspoon chili powder

1 tablespoon black pepper

1 tablespoon paprika

1 tablespoon plus 1 teaspoon garlic powder

1 tablespoon plus 1 teaspoon onion powder

1 tablespoon cumin

1 tablespoon plus 1 teaspoon oregano

1 tablespoon extra-virgin olive oil

1 onion, diced

4 garlic cloves, chopped

1 pound ground turkey or beef

½ cup cooking oil

¾ cup flour

32 ounces beef or chicken broth

1 cup roasted chili sauce (recipe follows)

French fries, homemade or store-bought

TO GARNISH

Grated Cheddar cheese

Chopped avocado

Tomatoes

Green onion

Sour cream

1 In a small bowl, mix chili powder, pepper, paprika, garlic powder, onion powder, cumin, and oregano, and set aside.

2 Heat olive oil over medium-high heat. Add onion and cook 5 minutes. Add garlic and cook 1 minute more. Add meat to mixture and break up. Add 1 tablespoon of seasoning blend to meat.

3 Cook meat about 5 minutes; drain if using beef. Transfer meat to slow cooker.

4 In a medium stock pot on medium-high heat, add cooking oil. When heated, add flour and whisk well until you achieve a light brown roux, about 4 minutes. Add rest of spice blend and whisk for about a minute. Add broth and whisk until well mixed. Add chili sauce and mix well.

5 Pour mixture over meat in slow cooker. Cover with a lid and cook on high for 4 hours or low for 8. The last hour of cooking time, cook uncovered.

6 Top french fries, hot out of the oven or fryer, with chili, and serve with grated Cheddar cheese, chopped avocado, tomatoes, green onion, and sour cream to garnish.

Recipe courtesy of
www.creolecontessa.com

ROASTED CHILE SAUCE

5 dried guajillo chiles

8 dried chile de árbol

1 pound tomatillos

10 serrano peppers, fresh, remove stems

2 jalapeños, fresh, remove stems

4 garlic cloves

1 white onion, quartered

Pinch of salt

1 tablespoon extra-virgin olive oil

1 small can of hot tomato sauce

1 Break open guajillo and chile de árbol to remove seeds. Discard seeds and add dried chiles to a small stock pot. Cover dried chiles with water and bring to a rolling boil. Turn off heat, cover pot, and let sit to rehydrate for at least 15 minutes.

2 Turn the oven on broil. In a baking pan, add tomatillos, serrano and jalapeños peppers, garlic, and onion. Add a pinch of salt and 1 tablespoon of olive oil. Broil just until tomatillos blister; watch carefully and remove from heat before they burst.

3 In a food processor or blender, add roasted vegetables including any liquid from pan, and rehydrated chiles. Process until smooth. Add hot tomato sauce to mixture and stir.

4 Take 1 cup of liquid gold chile sauce and set aside. Let remaining chile sauce cool, then freeze for later use.

 Recipe courtesy of www.creolecontessa.com

CHEESY RANCH POTATOES

SERVES 6

Cooking time: 5 to 6 hours on low

This absolutely perfect and easy side dish comes from one of the best food sites on the Net! Melissa Sperka of *Melissa's Southern Style Kitchen* is one of my favorite cooks of all times. Her recipes never fail to disappoint. Fact is, I love southern food and she does it up right. She's always telling me there has to be a little southern in me, and that's right—if you count South Brooklyn, New York.

1 can (10¾ ounces) cream of potato soup
1 can (10¾ ounces) cream of celery soup
8 ounces sour cream
1 cup chicken broth
6 tablespoons butter, melted
1 package (0.4 ounce) dry buttermilk ranch dressing mix
½ teaspoon black pepper
30 ounces shredded hashbrown potatoes, thawed
1 medium sweet onion, finely diced
3 cup shredded Colby-Jack cheese, divided
2 green onion for garnishing, thinly sliced

1 Spray the inside of a 6-quart slow cooker liberally with cooking spray.

2 In a large mixing bowl, whisk together the cream of potato soup, cream of celery soup, sour cream, chicken broth, butter, ranch dressing mix, and black pepper.

3 Add the thawed hashbrown potatoes, diced onion, and 2½ cups of the shredded Colby-Jack cheese. Mix until the potatoes are evenly coated. Pour into the slow cooker.

4 Cover the opening of the slow cooker with paper towels to absorb the condensation, then fit the lid tightly on top. The paper towels will prevent the condensation from dripping back into the potatoes making the sauce too thin.

5 Cook on low for 5 to 6 hours, until the potatoes are cooked through and tender. Uncover and sprinkle with the remaining shredded cheese. Once done, leave uncovered and let stand for 20 minutes prior to serving. Garnish with thinly sliced green onion.

Recipe courtesy of
www.melissassouthernstylekitchen.com

SLOW COOKER BAKED POTATOES

MAKES 10–12 SERVINGS

Cooking time: 8 hours on low

Here's a great technique for "baked potatoes" prepared in your slow cooker! These potatoes, and the great suggestions that make them a meal in themselves, come from my friend Claudia Lamascolo from *What's Cookin' Italian Style*. A transplanted New Yorker, Caudia now calls Florida home, but her heart is pure New York!

10 to 12 potatoes (I like to use red, white, or yellow potatoes), scrubbed
Salt and pepper
Softened butter, optional

1 Wash the potatoes, place on foil, prick with a fork, add salt and pepper, and spread with softened butter if desired. Fill the crock-pot with potatoes and cook on low (dry, no liquid). Prick with fork after 8 hours to check doneness.

2 Remove from slow cooker and slice open; fluff with a fork in the middle. Top as desired. You can use leftover chili, stews, or canned corned beef hash; add some shredded cheese for melting and your meal is complete.

SUGGESTED TOPPINGS

Greek-Style Potato: Feta cheese crumbles, olives, Greek dressing, shredded lettuce, and chopped tomatoes.

Philly-Style Potato: Steak slices topped with provolone, sautéed peppers, onions, and mushrooms.

Italian-Style Potato: Crushed meatballs in sauce topped with shredded mozzarella.

Pizza-Style Potato: Pepperoni, mozzarella. (Add sausage, mushrooms, peppers, or your favorite pizza toppings.)

 Recipe courtesy of www.whatscookinitalianstylecuisine.com

APPLE PIE CAKE

SERVES 6

Cooking time: 2 to 4 hours on high or 4 to 6 hours on low

Here's a moist coffee cake that's perfect for your slow cooker. A bonus: its autumnal aroma will scent your house like potpourri. This was something my mother made when she had apples, but not enough to make an apple pie. We all enjoyed it, especially with some whipped cream on top!

2 cups flour
1 teaspoon cinnamon
1 teaspoon nutmeg
⅛ teaspoon ground cloves, optional
1 teaspoon baking soda
½ teaspoon salt
4 tablespoons butter, softened
¾ cup sugar
1 egg
2 tablespoons water
1 teaspoon vanilla
2½ cups finely diced apple (about 3)
½ cup chopped nuts

1 Combine the flour, cinnamon, nutmeg, cloves (if using), baking soda, and salt. Set aside.

2 With an electric mixer, cream the butter and sugar until light and fluffy. Add the egg, water, and vanilla, beating well. Add the flour and spice mixture and blend well.

3 Stir in the apples and nuts.

4 Place in a well-greased 5-quart slow cooker.

5 Lay 2 to 3 paper towels over slow cooker and secure them with the lid (the lid will hold them in place). This is to prevent the condensation from ending up in the cobbler.

6 Cook on low 4 to 6 hours, or high 2 to 4 hours, or until a toothpick inserted in the center comes out clean.

APPLE DAPPLE PUDDING

SERVES 6 TO 8

Cooking time: 3 to 4 hours on high or 4 to 6 hours on low

My mom used to make something like this years ago. I think the original recipe came from an old Pillsbury Bake-Off cookbook from the early 1950s. I've updated it here with some convenience ingredients and adjusted for the slow cooker. These types of desserts are perfect for the slow cooker. You can always switch to the warm setting and leave it till you're ready to serve. This dessert is lucious warm with some heavy cream poured on top, in the British style (the Brits aren't big on whipped cream). Try it if you never have. It's wonderful!

4 to 5 medium Granny Smith (or variety of your choice) apples, peeled, cored, and sliced
1 cup apple cider or water
1 tablespoon lemon juice
2 tablespoons flour
½ teaspoon cinnamon
⅛ teaspoon nutmeg
⅓ cup sugar
¼ cup quick or old-fashioned oats
1 box (14 to 19 ounces) apple cinnamon muffin mix
½ cup butter, melted

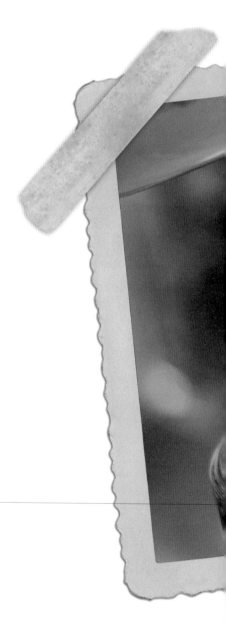

1 Peel, core, and slice apples (I used one of those combo corers/slicers so my slices were pretty thick).

2 Place apples in the crock of a 4- to 5-quart slow cooker. Add apple cider, lemon juice, flour, cinnamon, nutmeg, sugar, and oats and stir well, making sure all the apple slices are coated.

3 Top with muffin mix, reserving any included topping or crumb packet for future use. Drizzle melted butter over the top and poke batter in several places so that some of the muffin mix and butter is incorporated into the apple layer. I gave one or two rough stirs.

4 Cover and cook on low 4 to 6 hours or on high 3 to 4 hours, or until the pudding has the look and texture of moistened poultry stuffing and is springy to the touch.

147

BANANA BREAD

MAKES 8 SERVINGS

*Cooking time: 2 to 3 hours on high or
3 to 4 hours on high if cooking in a loaf pan*

Ever since childhood, this has been one of my favorite things to eat. I never would have dreamed you could bake it in your slow cooker until my sister schooled me on how to do it; her slow cooker banana bread is moist and lovely. One of the most important things you need to do is place paper towels under the lid to catch condensation. You can bake right in the insert, but if you have a pan that fits in the liner, that may be used as well.

2 cups flour
1 teaspoon baking soda
1 teaspoon salt
½ cup chopped nuts (pecans or walnuts)
¼ pound (1 stick) butter, softened
1 cup sugar
2 eggs
1 teaspoon vanilla
3 cups mashed ripe bananas (about 3 large)

1 Remove stoneware insert from slow cooker. Set slow cooker to high. Grease or spray the insert to a slow cooker or a metal or Pyrex loaf pan (9 x 5 x 4-inch). *Note*: Any shape baker or pan can be used as long as it fits in the crock pot and has the approximate volume of a loaf pan (about 2 quarts).

2 In a small bowl, mix flour, baking soda, salt, and nuts. Set aside.

3 In a medium bowl, beat butter and sugar until fluffy. Add eggs, one at a time, beating well after each addition. Beat in vanilla and the mashed bananas.

4 Gradually add the dry ingredients, stirring just enough to incorporate. Do not overmix.

5 Pour batter either into the prepared stoneware insert or the prepared pan. If using a loaf pan, either place a rack in the stoneware insert or use crumpled foil to keep pan from touching the bottom of the crock. Place pan or stoneware insert into the crock pot sleeve. Place 2 layers of paper towels over top of crock and cover (lid will secure the papers towels and prevent them from falling into crock).

6 Cook on high for about 2 to 3 hours (if cooking in the insert itself) or 3 to 4 hours if cooking in the loaf pan.

CHERRY COBBLER

SERVES 10 TO 12

Cooking time: 3 to 5 hours on high or 5 to 8 hours on low

You'd never believe that this luscious cherry dessert is made entirely from convenience products. All it takes is some cake mix, canned pie filling, nuts, butter, and water and you're good to go. The family is guaranteed to love this. Great for Valentine's Day!

2 cans (21 ounces each) cherry pie filling
1 box (18.25 ounces) yellow cake mix
½ cup toasted, sliced almonds
¼ pound (1 stick) butter, melted
1 tablespoon water

1 Spray the crock of a 5-quart (or larger) slow cooker with non-stick spray.

2 Add cherry pie filling to the slow cooker. Distribute the cake mix over the cherries. Add the toasted almonds.

3 Drizzle melted butter over the cake mix. Run a knife through the layers as if you were making a marble cake—do *not* mix the ingredients, simply marble them. Sprinkle the water over the top.

4 Lay 2 to 3 paper towels over slow cooker and secure them with the lid (the lid will hold them in place). This is to catch condensation.

5 Cook on high 3 to 5 hours, or low 5 to 8 hours, or until cake parts are set and not sticky.

TROPICAL AMBROSIA DUMP CAKE

SERVES ABOUT 8

Cooking time: 4 to 6 hours on high or 6 to 8 hours on low

Here's a dump cake with the taste of the tropics! I am a huge fan of anything coconut and especially if it's mixed with pineapple. A couple of cans of fruit, a cake mix, and some coconut are pretty much all you need here. If you can't find pineapple-flavored cake mix, yellow will do just fine.

1 can (15 ounces) tropical fruit salad
1 can (20 ounces) crushed pineapple
½ cup maraschino cherries
½ cup shredded coconut
1 box (16.5 ounces) pineapple cake mix
¼ pound (1 stick) unsalted butter, melted

1 Spray a 4- to 6-quart slow cooker with non-stick spray.

2 Add the cans of fruit (including liquid), cherries, and coconut to the slow cooker; stir to combine.

3 Pour cake mix over fruit. Drizzle melted butter on top of cake mix.

4 Cover and cook on high 4 to 6 hours, or on low 6 to 8 hours. Serve warm.

CHOCOLATE CHERRY COBBLER

SERVES 6

Cooking time: 2 to 3 hours on high or 4 to 5 hours on low

Cracker Barrel restaurant serves up a famous one of these, and several "copycat" recipes are circulating online. My slow-cooker adaptation includes extra chocolate and, of course, nuts.

1 can (21 ounces) cherry pie filling
1½ cups flour
½ cup sugar
2 teaspoons baking powder
½ teaspoon salt
¼ cup (½ stick) butter
1 cup (6 ounce bag) chocolate chips
¼ cup evaporated milk
1 egg
½ cup slivered almonds

1 Spread cherry pie filling in the bottom of a 4- to 6-quart slow cooker.

2 Mix flour, sugar, baking powder, and salt in a medium bowl.

3 Cut butter into chunks and add to the flour mixture. Cut in butter until the flour mixture resembles small peas. Set aside.

4 Melt chocolate chips either in the microwave or stovetop. Stir frequently until mixture is smooth. Cool for about 5 minutes. Add evaporated milk and egg to melted chocolate. Stir until well blended.

5 Add the chocolate mixture to the flour mixture. Mix very well. Drop randomly on top of cherry filling in baking dish. Sprinkle with the almonds.

6 Cook for about 5 hours on low, 3 hours on high. (Times are approximate; check at 4 hours if using low heat, and at 2 hours if using high heat.)

7 Serve warm with ice cream, whipped cream, or poured cream.

BLUEBERRY COBBLER

MAKES 6 SERVINGS

Cooking time: 2 to 2½ hours on high

Blueberries have made headlines in recent years for their substantial health benefits. But as spring and summer desserts go, nothing is more timeless than a blueberry cobbler. This delicious recipe comes from my friend Ronda Eagle of *Kitchen Dreaming*. Ronda's family has been enjoying this dessert for quite some time, and she wanted to share it with all of you!

1¼ cups all-purpose flour, divided
1 cup sugar, divided
1 teaspoon baking powder
1 egg, lightly beaten
¼ cup milk
1 teaspoon vanilla
2 tablespoons canola oil
⅛ teaspoon salt
Grated lemon zest and juice of one lemon
4 cups fresh or frozen blueberries
2 tablespoons butter, cut into small pieces

1 Spray a slow cooker with nonstick cooking spray or line with a crock pot liner.

2 In a large bowl, combine 1 cup of the flour, 2 tablespoons of the sugar, and the baking powder. In a separate bowl combine the egg, milk, vanilla, and oil; stir into dry ingredients just until moistened to avoid overworking the batter. The batter will be thick.

3 In a large bowl, combine salt, the remaining flour and sugar, and lemon zest and juice; add blueberries and toss to coat. Pour into the bottom of the slow cooker and top with butter.

4 With your hands or a spoon, drop batter in portions on top of the fruit in the slow cooker.

5 Cover and cook on high for 2 to 2½ hours, until the topping has puffed and the fruit is bubbling. A toothpick inserted into cobbler dough should come out clean.

6 Serve warm with whipped cream or ice cream; garnish with a sprig of mint if desired.

 Recipe courtesy of www.kitchendreaming.com

DONUT BREAD PUDDING

SERVES ABOUT 8

Cooking time: 4 hours on high or 6 to 8 hours on low

A big fall treat in my area of upstate New York—in the heart of apple country—is apple cider donuts, which are only available for about two months of the year. My nephew happened to be visiting me during this time, so to introduce him to this particular treat I bought 2 boxes of the donuts; for some reason, though, we only ate the first box. By the time I discovered the second box, they were stale. Not wanting to throw them out, I decided to experiment and made bread pudding. The recipe was a huge hit when I served it for a small dinner party. I am sure you'll love it too. Don't have donuts? No problem—substitute bread and donut spices!

6 to 8 cake donuts (see Note)
4 eggs
5 cups milk
¾ cup sugar
½ teaspoon nutmeg
⅛ teaspoon mace

1 Cut donuts into small pieces of about 1 inch. Place in crockpot.

2 In a large bowl, beat eggs. Whisk in the milk, sugar, and spices. Pour over donuts in crock pot.

3 Cover and cook on high for 4 hours, low for 6 to 8 hours.

Note: Make sure to use cake donuts, not the raised type. Or you can use day-old French or Italian bread, but increase the sugar to 1 cup, the nutmeg to 1 teaspoon, and the mace to ¼ teaspoon—these 2 spices are the standard "donut" spices, so the overall pudding will taste like cake donuts.

LEMON BARS

YIELD VARIES AS TO SIZE/SHAPE COOKER USED. THE CASSEROLE CROCK YIELDED 12 BARS.

Cooking time: 2 to 3 hours on high

I've always loved lemon bars. Trouble is, too often when you get the craving for them, you're out of fresh lemons. At least that's the case here. But if you keep one convenience item in stock, you'll always be prepared to whip them up. Lemon curd, whether store-bought or homemade, fills the bill nicely. Be sure to put paper towels under the lid when cooking these, to catch condensation (which will otherwise spoil your lemon bars).

¼ pound plus 4 tablespoons (1½ sticks) unsalted butter, softened
½ cup sugar
¼ teaspoon salt
1 egg
1 tablespoon lemon zest
½ teaspoon vanilla
2 cups flour
1 jar (10 to 12 ounces) lemon curd
Confectioners' sugar for dusting

1 Beat the butter and sugar in a large bowl with an electric mixer.

2 Add the salt, egg, lemon zest, and vanilla; beat well. With the mixer at low speed, add the flour 1 cup at a time. Beat only until a soft dough forms.

3 Press dough into the crock of a 9 x 13-inch casserole slow cooker (preferred) or a 6- to 7-quart oval slow cooker. Spread lemon curd evenly on top of dough.

4 Place 2 layers of paper towels over the top of the crock and cover with lid. The lid will secure the paper towels and prevent them from falling on the lemon bars.

5 Set slow cooker to high and cook for 2 to 3 hours (mine took 3 in the casserole crock). Bars are done when the corners (edges) are beginning to brown and the center is set. Bars will continue to cook during the cooling.

6 Cool completely in the slow cooker. Cut into bars and dust with confectioners' sugar.

DULCE DE LECHE

MAKES ¾ CUP

*Cooking time: 4 to 6 hours on high
and 6 to 8 hours cooling on off*

I love dulce de leche so much, I am happy to eat it straight from the jar with a spoon! But this has so many uses really—as an ingredient in sweet treats, as a sauce or topping, and even as a breakfast food. I read that one of the most popular breakfasts in Argentina is sliced green apples dipped in dulce de leche. What a great way to start the day! Dulce de leche is so easy to make—just submerge a can of condensed milk in water and let your slow cooker work its magic.

1 to 2 cans sweetened condensed milk
2 cups water

1. Line slow cooker with aluminum foil or use a slow-cooker bag.

2. Open can(s) of condensed milk and cover with aluminum foil. Place 2 cups of water in slow cooker. Place cans in the water. Cook on high for at least 4 hours (produces a lighter product) or up to 6 hours (produces a darker, richer product).

3. Shut off slow cooker and allow contents to come to room temperature. *Do not uncover slow cooker during cooling!* This will take at least 6 to 8 hours.

4. Remove dulce de leche from cans and store in either plastic or glass containers. Refrigerate product until use.

Note: You can make as much as you wish; procedure is the same, only the number of cans of condensed milk will vary.

MOM'S RICE PUDDING

SERVES 6

Cooking time: 1⅓ hours on high or 3 to 4 hours on low

This was our traditional Friday dessert when I was growing up. Mom discovered the recipe on a box of rice and it became her go-to recipe for rice pudding. She'd prepare hers in the oven, and it had a long cook time. Which makes it perfect for the slow cooker. It's a dessert that will free up your oven for other things. This is the creamiest rice pudding I have ever tasted. We never put cinnamon or raisins in it because the taste by itself is great, but add about a teaspoon of cinnamon and up to ½ cup of raisins if you like. Toasted nuts on top are wonderful.

⅓ cup uncooked long-grain rice
⅓ cup sugar
1 teaspoon vanilla extract
4 cups (1 quart) whole milk (no substitutions)

Place all ingredients in a 4- to 6-quart lightly greased slow cooker. Stir well until sugar dissolves. Cover and cook on low 3 to 4 hours, or high 1⅓ hours or until milk is absorbed.

SLOW COOKER BROWNIES

MAKES 6 TO 8 SERVINGS

Cooking time: 4 hours on low

These are some awesome brownies—and you'd never believe they're made in the crock pot! My friend Claudia Lamascolo from *What's Cookin' Italian Style Cuisine* has won so many contests for her chocolate desserts, I lost count. These brownies can be made plain or dressed up with frosting.

1¼ cup flour
¼ cup unsweetened cocoa powder
¾ teaspoon baking powder
½ teaspoon salt
¼ pound (1 stick) unsalted butter, cut into pieces
8 ounces bittersweet chocolate, chopped
1 cup sugar
3 large eggs, lightly beaten
1 cup walnuts, coarsely chopped
1 cup semisweet chocolate chips

1 Spray a 5-quart crock pot (slow cooker) with cooking spray. Line the bottom with parchment paper to fit and lightly spray the paper.

2 In a small bowl, mix together flour, cocoa powder, baking powder, and salt.

3 Put butter and bittersweet chocolate in microwave-safe bowl and heat in 30-second intervals, stirring, until the chocolate is melted. Add sugar, stir to combine. Add eggs and flour mixture, walnuts, and chocolate chips, and stir until moistened. Do not overmix. Carefully pour into slow cooker and smooth top of batter with a spatula.

4 Cover and cook on low for 3½ hours. Then uncover and cook an additional 30 minutes. Remove the crock and run a knife around the edge to loosen. Let cool at least 2 hours.

5 Flip onto cutting board, peel off the parchment paper, and cut into squares. Frost them or serve plain or with your favorite ice cream, whipped cream, and hot fudge on top.

Recipe courtesy of
www.whatscookinitalianstylecuisine.com

PEANUT BUTTER CUP TRIFLE

Don't forget those slow cookers come holiday-party time. They are perfect for a dessert-bar buffet. This delicious and decadent trifle isn't made in the slow cooker, of course, but some components are. Get creative with your own serving ideas. The possibilities are endless.

Brownies, cut into cubes (previous recipe)
Ready-to-serve vanilla pudding
Mini peanut butter cups, cut into quarters
Whipped topping
Peanut butter caramel sauce (recipe follows)

The amount to include of each element is up to you, since this trifle comes together as guests assemble their own at a buffet, layering the ingredients atop brownies. Amounts will be determined by how many you are serving and their appetites.

PEANUT BUTTER CARAMEL SAUCE

MAKES 1 CUP

This peanuty sauce will have them coming back for more! The sauce is made on the stovetop, but when transferred to a small slow cooker, it's a great addition to a dessert bar. Guests can help themselves and ladle it over their desserts. Just keep the slow cooker on warm and watch this sauce disappear!

½ cup creamy peanut butter
½ cup heavy cream
¼ cup brown sugar
2 tablespoons light corn syrup

Mix all ingredients in a small saucepan. Heat over medium heat until sugar is dissolved and bubbles form around the edge of the sauce.

Index

A

Ale Cheese Soup, Steak &, 36–37
Ale Short Ribs, Cream &, 90–91
Aloha Pineapple Sauce, 19
appetizers
  Aloha Pineapple Sauce, 19
  Asian Orange Chicken Wings, 18–19
  Chex Snack Mix, 22–23
  Hot Jalapeño & Chile Popper Dip, 24–25
  Smoky Pimento Cheese Queso Dip, 20–21
apples
  Apple Butter BBQ Ribs, 62–63
  Apple Dapple Pudding, 146–47
  Apple Pie Cake, 144–45
apricot preserves, in Fruity BBQ Chicken, 54–55
Asian BBQ Beef Strips, 84–85
Asian Orange Chicken Wings, 18–19

B

bacon
  Cheesy Bacon Chicken & Taters, 46–47
  Hot German Potato Salad, 132–33
  Stuffed Beef Rolls, 110–11
Baked Potatoes, Slow Cooker, 140–41
Banana Bread, 148–49
barley, in Beef Barley Soup, 28–29
BBQ Chicken, Fruity, 54–55
BBQ Ribs, Apple Butter, 62–63
beans and legumes
  Chili Hater's Chili, 114–15
  Hearty Northeast Bean Soup, 30–31
  Smoked Sausage & Lentil Soup, 34–35
  Split Pea Soup with Ham, 38–39
beef
  Asian BBQ Beef Strips, 84–85
  Beef Barley Soup, 28–29
  Beef Stroganoff, 94–95
  Braised Short Ribs, 86–87
  Braised Steak, 96–97
  Classic Pot Roast, 78–79
  Classic Pot Roast with Veggies, 80–81
  Cream & Ale Short Ribs, 90–91
  Fruited Short Ribs, 92–93
  Ginger Beef with Mandarin Oranges, 98–99
  Maple-Glazed Short Ribs, 88–89
  Mississippi Swiss Steak, 104–5
  Orange Beef with Fire Peppers, 106–7
  Roasted Beef, 82–83
  Sichuan Beef with Carrots, 108–9
  Steak & Ale Cheese Soup, 36–37
  Stuffed Beef Rolls, 110–11
  Swiss Steak, 102–3
beef, ground
  Cheeseburger Soup, 32–33
  Chili Hater's Chili, 114–15
  Chopped Steak with Onion Mushroom Gravy, 100–101
  Creamy Penne, 124–25
  Five-Cheese Lasagna, 120–21
  Maple Meat Loaf, 112–13
  Spaghetti & Meat Sauce, 122–23
  Spicy Roasted Chili Cheese Fries, 136–37
beer
  Cream & Ale Short Ribs, 90–91
  in Roasted Beef, 82–83
  Steak & Ale Cheese Soup, 36–37
bell peppers
  Chili Hater's Chili, 114–15
  Orange Beef with Fire Peppers, 106–7
Blueberry Cobbler, 156–57
Braised Short Ribs, 86–87
Braised Steak, 96–97
bread
  Banana Bread, 148–49
  Country White Croutons, 20
Bread Pudding, Donut, 158–59
Brownies, Slow Cooker, 165
Brown Sugar Country-Style Pork Ribs, 64–65

C

cakes. See coffee cake; Dump Cake
Calypso Pork Chops, 70–71
Candied Acorn Squash, 128

Candied Baby Carrots, 129
carrots
    Candied Baby Carrots, 129
    Classic Pot Roast with Veggies, 80–81
    in Maple-Kissed Roasted Chicken, 42–43
    Sichuan Beef with Carrots, 108–9
cheese
    Baked Ziti, 118–19
    Cheeseburger Soup, 32–33
    Cheese & Potato Stuffed Pork Chops, 68–69
    Cheesy Bacon Chicken & Taters, 46–47
    Cheesy Hashbrown Casserole, 134
    Cheesy Ranch Potatoes, 139
    Cheesy Sausage & Taters, 75
    Creamy Penne, 124–25
    Hot Jalapeño & Chile Popper Dip, 24–25
    Smoky Pimento Cheese Queso Dip, 20–21
    Steak & Ale Cheese Soup, 36–37
cherries
    Cherry Cobbler, 150–51
    Chocolate Cherry Cobbler, 154–55
    dried, in Fruited Short Ribs, 92–93
Chex Snack Mix, 22–23
chicken
    Cheesy Bacon Chicken & Taters, 46–47
    Chicken & Noodles, 49
    Chicken Stroganoff, 48
    Chicken with Creamy Mushroom Rice,
        50–51
    Chicken with Vegetables, 52–53
    Fruity BBQ Chicken, 54–55
    Maple-Kissed Roasted Chicken, 42–43
    Roasted Drumsticks, 44
    Teriyaki Chicken, 56–57
chile peppers
    Chili Hater's Chili, 114–15
    Five-Cheese Lasagna, 120–21
    Hot Jalapeño & Chile Popper Dip, 24–25
    Mississippi Swiss Steak, 104–5
    Roasted Chile Sauce, 138
    Smoky Pimento Cheese Queso Dip, 20–21
Chili Cheese Fries, Spicy Roasted, 136–37

Chili Hater's Chili, 114–15
chocolate
    Chocolate Cherry Cobbler, 154–55
    in Peanut Butter Cup Trifle, 166
    Slow Cooker Brownies, 165
Chopped Steak with Onion Mushroom Gravy,
        100–101
Citrus Greek Potatoes, 130–31
cobblers
    Blueberry, 156–57
    Cherry, 150–51
    Chocolate Cherry, 154–55
    See also Dump Cake
coconut, in Tropical Ambrosia Dump Cake,
        152–53
coffee cake
    Apple Pie Cake, 144–45
Country-Style Pork Ribs, Brown Sugar,
        64–65
Cream & Ale Short Ribs, 90–91
Croutons, Country White, 20

D

desserts. See sweet treats
dips
    Hot Jalapeño & Chile Popper, 24–25
    Smoky Pimento Cheese Queso, 20–21
Donut Bread Pudding, 158–59
Dulce de Leche, 162–63
Dump Cake, Tropical Ambrosia, 152–53

F

Five-Cheese Lasagna, 120–21
Fruited Short Ribs, 92–93
Fruity BBQ Chicken, 54–55

G

ginger
    Ginger Beef with Mandarin Oranges, 98–99
    in Teriyaki Chicken, 56–57
gravies
    Golden Ranch, 74

Onion and Mushroom, 101

whiskey gravy, 67

green beans, in Chicken with Vegetables, 52–53

H

ham

Hearty Northeast Bean Soup, 30–31

Split Pea Soup with, 38–39

Hashbrown Casserole, Cheesy, 134

Hot German Potato Salad, 132–33

J

Jalapeño & Chile Popper Dip, Hot, 24–25

L

Lasagna, Five-Cheese, 120–21

Lemon Bars, 160–61

Lentil Soup, Smoked Sausage &, 34–35

M

maple

Juicy Maple Pork with Sweet Potatoes, 60–61

Maple-Glazed Short Ribs, 88–89

Maple-Kissed Roasted Chicken, 42–43

Maple Meat Loaf, 112–13

Maple & Sage Seasoning Rub, 61

marinades

Aloha Pineapple Sauce, 19

Meat Loaf, Maple, 112–13

Mississippi Ribs, 66–67

Mississippi Swiss Steak, 104–5

Mom's Rice Pudding, 164

mushrooms

Beef Stroganoff, 94–95

Chicken Stroganoff, 48

Chicken with Creamy Mushroom Rice, 50–51

Onion Mushroom Gravy, 101

Pork Chop Stroganoff, 72–73

Swiss Steak, 102–3

N

Northeast Bean Soup, Hearty, 30–31

nuts. *See* peanut butter; peanuts

O

oranges

Asian Orange Chicken Wings, 18–19

Citrus Greek Potatoes, 130–31

Ginger Beef with Mandarin Oranges, 98–99

Orange Beef with Fire Peppers, 106–7

P

pasta and noodles

Baked Ziti, 118–19

Chicken & Noodles, 49

Creamy Penne, 124–25

Five-Cheese Lasagna, 120–21

Spaghetti & Meat Sauce, 122–23

peanut butter

Peanut Butter Caramel Sauce, 167

Peanut Butter Cup Trifle, 166

peanuts, in Chex Snack Mix, 22–23

Penne, Creamy, 124–25

Pimento Cheese Queso Dip, Smoky, 20–21

pineapple

Aloha Pineapple Sauce, 19

in Calypso Pork Chops, 70–71

Tropical Ambrosia Dump Cake, 152–53

pork

Apple Butter BBQ Ribs, 62–63

Brown Sugar Country-Style Pork Ribs, 64–65

Calypso Pork Chops, 70–71

Cheese & Potato Stuffed Pork Chops, 68–69

Cheesy Sausage & Taters, 75

Juicy Maple Pork with Sweet Potatoes, 60–61

Maple & Sage Seasoning Rub, 61

Mississippi Ribs, 66–67

Pork Chop Stroganoff, 72–73

Pork Chops with Golden Ranch Gravy, 74

See also bacon; ham; sausage

potatoes
    Baked Potatoes, Slow Cooker, 140–41
    Cheeseburger Soup, 32–33
    Cheese & Potato Stuffed Pork Chops, 68–69
    Cheesy Bacon Chicken & Taters, 46–47
    Cheesy Ranch Potatoes, 139
    Cheesy Sausage & Taters, 75
    Chicken with Vegetables, 52–53
    Citrus Greek Potatoes, 130–31
    Classic Pot Roast with Veggies, 80–81
    Hot German Potato Salad, 132–33
    Juicy Maple Pork with Sweet Potatoes,
      60–61
    Spicy Roasted Chili Cheese Fries, 136–37
Pot Roast, Classic, 78–79
Pot Roast with Veggies, Classic, 80–81
pretzels, in Chex Snack Mix, 22–23
puddings
    Apple Dapple Pudding, 146–47
    Donut Bread Pudding, 158–59
    Mom's Rice Pudding, 164

R

Ranch Seasoning Mix, 53
Rice, Creamy Mushroom, Chicken with,
    50–51
Rice Pudding, Mom's, 164
Roasted Beef, 82–83
Roasted Chili Sauce, 136
Roasted Drumsticks, 44

S

Sage Seasoning Rub, Maple &, 61
sandwiches
    Asian BBQ Beef Strips, 84–85
sauces
    Aloha Pineapple, 19
    apple butter, 62
    Dulce de Leche, 162–63
    meat sauce, 123
    orange sauce, 18
    Peanut Butter Caramel, 167

    Roasted Chile, 138
    sweet and tangy brown sugar, 64
    See also gravies
sausage
    Cheesy Hashbrown Casserole, 134
    Cheesy Sausage & Taters, 75
    Creamy Penne, 124–25
    Five-Cheese Lasagna, 120–21
    Hearty Northeast Bean Soup, 30–31
    Maple Meat Loaf, 112–13
    Sausage & Lentil Soup, Smoked, 34–35
seasonings
    Creole Seasoning Blend, 45
    Maple & Sage Seasoning Rub, 61
    meat seasoning rub, 62
    Ranch Seasoning Mix, 53
sherry, in Swiss Steak, 102–3
short ribs
    Braised, 86–87
    Cream & Ale, 90–91
    Fruited, 92–93
    Maple-Glazed, 88–89
Sichuan Beef with Carrots, 108–9
side dishes
    Candied Acorn Squash, 128
    Candied Baby Carrots, 129
    Cheesy Hashbrown Casserole, 134
    Cheesy Ranch Potatoes, 139
    Citrus Greek Potatoes, 130–31
    Hot German Potato Salad, 132–33
    Roasted Chile Sauce, 138
    Slow Cooker Baked Potatoes, 140–41
    Spicy Roasted Chili Cheese Fries, 136–37
slow cookers, choosing and using, 13–15
Smoky Pimento Cheese Queso Dip, 20–21
soups
    Beef Barley Soup, 28–29
    Cheeseburger Soup, 32–33
    Hearty Northeast Bean Soup, 30–31
    Smoked Sausage & Lentil Soup, 34–35
    Split Pea Soup with Ham, 38–39
    Steak & Ale Cheese Soup, 36–37

sour cream
    Beef Stroganoff, 94–95
    Cheesy Ranch Potatoes, 139
soy sauce, in Teriyaki Chicken, 56–57
Spaghetti & Meat Sauce, 122–23
Spicy Roasted Chili Cheese Fries, 136–37
Split Pea Soup with Ham, 38–39
Squash, Candied Acorn, 128
Steak & Ale Cheese Soup, 36–37
stroganoff
    Beef, 94–95
    Chicken, 48
    Pork Chop, 72–73
Stuffed Beef Rolls, 110–11
sweetened condensed milk, in Dulce de Leche, 162–63
Sweet Potatoes, Juicy Maple Pork with, 60–61
sweet treats
    Apple Dapple Pudding, 146–47
    Apple Pie Cake, 142–43, 144–45
    Banana Bread, 148–49
    Blueberry Cobbler, 156–57
    Cherry Cobbler, 150–51
    Chocolate Cherry Cobbler, 154–55
    Donut Bread Pudding, 158–59
    Dulce de Leche, 162–63
    Lemon Bars, 160–61
    Mom's Rice Pudding, 164
    Peanut Butter Caramel Sauce, 167
    Peanut Butter Cup Trifle, 166
    Slow Cooker Brownies, 165
    Tropical Ambrosia Dump Cake, 152–53
Swiss Steak, 102–3
Swiss Steak, Mississippi, 104–5

T

Teriyaki Chicken, 56–57
tomatillos, in Roasted Chile Sauce, 138
tomatoes
    Chili Hater's Chili, 114–15
    Creamy Penne, 124–25
    Spaghetti & Meat Sauce, 122–23
Trifle, Peanut Butter Cup, 166
Tropical Ambrosia Dump Cake, 152–53
turkey, ground, in Spicy Roasted Chili Cheese Fries, 136–37

W

wine, in Roasted Beef, 82–83

Z

Ziti, Baked, 118–19